Mastering IDoc Business Scenarios with SAP® NetWeaver PI

 PRESS

SAP PRESS is a joint initiative of SAP and Galileo Press. The know-how offered by SAP specialists combined with the expertise of the Galileo Press publishing house offers the reader expert books in the field. SAP PRESS features first-hand information and expert advice, and provides useful skills for professional decision-making.

SAP PRESS offers a variety of books on technical and business related topics for the SAP user. For further information, please visit our website: *www.sap-press.com*.

Jim Hagemann Snabe, Ann Rosenberg, Charles Møller, Mark Scavillo
Business Process Management – the SAP Roadmap
2009, 411 pp.
ISBN 978-1-59229-231-8

Martin Huvar, Timm Falter, Thomas Fiedler, Alexander Zubev
Developing Applications with Enterprise SOA
2008, 329 pp.
ISBN 978-1-59229-178-6

Karl-Heinz Kühnhauser
Discover ABAP
2008, 503 pp.
ISBN 978-1-59229-152-6

Horst Keller, Sascha Krüger
ABAP Objects
2nd revised and extended edition 2007, 1059 pp., with DVD
ISBN 978-1-59229-079-6

Michał Krawczyk, Michał Kowalczewski

Mastering IDoc Business Scenarios with SAP® NetWeaver PI

Galileo Press

Bonn • Boston

Galileo Press is named after the Italian physicist, mathematician and philosopher Galileo Galilei (1564–1642). He is known as one of the founders of modern science and an advocate of our contemporary, heliocentric worldview. His words Eppur si muove (And yet it moves) have become legendary. The Galileo Press logo depicts Jupiter orbited by the four Galilean moons, which were discovered by Galileo in 1610.

Editors Stefan Proksch, Maike Lübbers
Copy Editor Jutta VanStean
Cover Design Nadine Kohl
Photo Credit Masterfile/RF
Layout Design Vera Brauner
Production Iris Warkus
Typesetting SatzPro, Krefeld (Germany)
Printed and bound in Canada

ISBN 978-1-59229-288-2

© 2010 by Galileo Press Inc., Boston (MA)
2nd Edition, updated and revised 2010

Contents

Preface

This book is based on our experiences with IDoc scenarios and using SAP NetWeaver Process Integration (SAP NetWeaver PI, formerly known as SAP Exchange Infrastructure/SAP XI). This is the second edition of this book and quite a few new functionalities are described such as new IDoc packaging options, IDoc monitoring using SAP Solution Manager, the ALE distribution model, and sending IDoc messages using ABAP proxies.

IDocs still provide one of the most popular interfaces to enable the connection of SAP application systems (SAP R/3, SAP ERP) to both third-party and other SAP application systems. They can be easily generated from many application transactions and used to generate various documents in SAP application systems, in all possible modules and solutions.

> **Note**
>
> Most of the screens are taken from SAP NetWeaver PI 7.0 but the exact same functionality also exists in SAP NetWeaver PI 7.1, the latest release currently available. Some functionality also requires enhancement package 1 for SAP NetWeaver, such as sender IDoc adapter packaging.

With the introduction of SAP NetWeaver PI it became much easier to use IDocs in the new XML world. SAP NetWeaver PI allows flexible integration using IDocs in standard form, with very little configuration needed to create a simple IDoc message flow.

Based on our experience, we assert that IDoc integration flows can be very efficient if they are well designed. This book explains both the concepts behind IDocs and how to process IDocs via SAP NetWeaver PI. Readers will gain comprehensive knowledge of all possible scenarios of IDoc flows, as this book covers many real solutions based on our integration project experience. This book is structured as follows:

Chapter 1 provides details on how to prepare an SAP system for an IDoc-enabled configuration. It deals with the technical aspects of the configuration, such as connections and ports.

Chapter 2 shows you how to configure input and output IDocs in certain business scenarios. Due to capacity restrictions, we focus only on the most common scenarios from Materials Management (MM) and Sales and Distribution (SD).

Chapter 3 shows a new scenario—master data distribution—which includes a description of the ALE distribution model configuration.

Chapter 4 details administrator tasks connected with IDoc monitoring, dealing with errors and reprocessing on the SAP side. The second edition also contains monitoring IDoc scenarios using both SAP Solution Manager and Computer Center Management System (CCMS).

Chapter 5 is dedicated to the IDoc exchange using SAP NetWeaver PI. In this chapter, we cover everything from standard configuration of IDoc flows through SAP NetWeaver PI to more advanced topics such as IDoc packaging and IDoc mappings. The second edition also contains new functionalities such as ALE acknowledgment messages sent as SAP PI request messages (one of the latest enhancements introduced with SAP enhancement package 1 for SAP NetWeaver), sender IDoc adapter packaging, and a description of a solution that allows you to send IDocs as ABAP proxy messages.

Chapter 6 provides a short summary of all of the ideas described in the book.

The Appendix contains a list of the most important qualifiers used with one of the most popular IDocs, ORDERS05. This IDoc is used for many business scenarios such as sales order/purchase order exchanges and updates.

Acknowledgments

Michał Krawczyk thanks his family for their never-ending encouragement and inspiration for his work.

Michał Kowalczewski thanks his family and friends for their love and support.

Both authors thank their colleagues from the integration team at BCC for their ideas and support. Together, we have developed many integration scenarios and these gave us new ideas on how to handle integration more efficiently.

Both authors also thank their editors Stefan Proksch and Maike Lübbers at Galileo Press for their support in preparing this book.

1   IDoc Basics and Elemental Technical Configuration

Intermediate documents (IDocs) are data containers (messages) with predefined structures, used to exchange information between SAP application systems and the external world. Each message has its own type, which usually corresponds to a business transaction. IDocs are exchanged as asynchronous messages in two ways:

▶ **Outbound IDocs**
These IDocs are sent from the SAP system. They are created either from business transactions (as in the creation of a sales order) or from master data (such as materials or business partners) and sent to an external system. Configuration of outbound and inbound IDocs coming from business transactions is explained in Chapter 2 and IDocs coming from master data is described in Chapter 3.

▶ **Inbound IDocs**
IDocs of this kind are received by the SAP system and create business transactions or master data.

An IDoc has a specific *IDoc type* that corresponds to the message structure and also a *message type* that is related more closely to a business transaction. An IDoc type can transfer several message types. A list and definitions of standard IDoc/message types are available from *http://ifr.sap.com/catalog/query.asp*.

An IDoc type (*IDoc definition*) consists of segments that contain fields. Segments can be mandatory or optional and can occur once or more than once. It is also possible that one segment can contain other segments, as in a *tree structure*. The number and format of the segments can vary for each IDoc type, but every IDoc has a *control record segment*. The structure of the control record segment is identical in all IDoc types. The segment is used to describe the sender, receiver, and the meaning of a message, and is used for entering the IDoc in the system, as explained in Section 1.3. Figure 1.1 shows the structure of a generic IDoc.

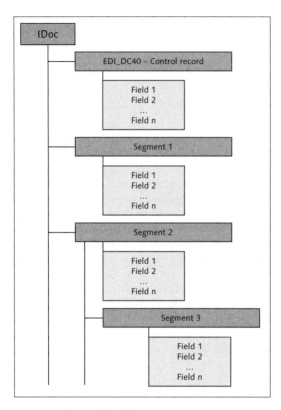

Figure 1.1 Generic IDoc Structure

To become more familiar with the IDoc type, you can open Transaction WE60, press [F4] at the IDoc TYPE field, and look for available types. Then, enter "INVOIC02" or "ORDERS05" in this field, press [F8], and look at the IDoc's structure.

To build an IDoc exchange scenario, you first have to complete the technical steps needed for further business system customizing. These mandatory steps are as follows:

▸ Setting the connections to other systems, known as *remote function call* (RFC) destinations (see Section 1.1).

▸ Maintaining ports as the transmission medium (see Section 1.2).

▸ Maintaining the *partner profiles* needed to distinguish different messages and their destinations (see Section 1.3).

In the next section, we provide details on connecting SAP systems with other systems.

1.1 Creating Connections Between Different Systems

In this section, we will explain how to connect your SAP application system to another SAP application system or to an external system, such as a vendor's CRM system.

1.1.1 RFC Type Connection

The first example will show how to connect an SAP ERP Central Component (SAP ECC) system to another SAP ECC system. Connections to other SAP application systems and to non-SAP systems are defined in Transaction SM59. After you start the transaction, you can choose between different connection types, as shown in Figure 1.2.

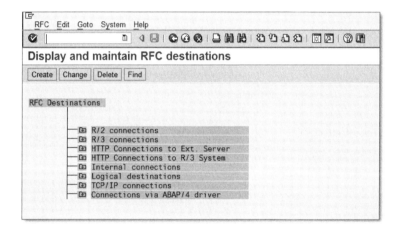

Figure 1.2 Initial Screen of Transaction SM59

Each of these types represents a different connection method and requires various parameters to be set, as follows:

▶ **SAP R/2 connections**
The R/2 type is rarely used today. As the name indicates, it is used only for SAP R/2 communication.

▶ **HTTP connections to external servers and to the R/3 system**
It is possible to use the most common Internet protocol: *hypertext transfer protocol* (HTTP). This is particularly useful for communicating directly via the Internet without special rules concerning firewalls.

► **Internal connections**

Internal connections specify the ABAP system connected to the same database as the current system. These entries are predefined and cannot be modified. However, the internal connections work as aliases for others. In such connections, some data from the original—such as logon information—could be overwritten.

► **Logical destinations**

This type works as an alias to another R/3 connection. Host data is copied, and the only thing that needs to be specified is the logon information: login, password, client, and language.

► **TCP/IP connections**

Transmission Control Protocol/Internet Protocol (TCP/IP) connections are used by external programs to communicate with the RFC library.

► **SAP R/3 connections**

This type is used for establishing connections to other SAP application systems—such as SAP R/3 or SAP ECC—that are based on SAP NetWeaver Application Server (SAP NetWeaver AS). To set up a connection, you need the same set of parameters as you do when you configure access to an SAP application system via SAP logon. These include the host name, system number, client, login, password, and language.

To create a new RFC destination of type R/3 you have to enter parameters common to all connection types, as follows:

► **RFC destination**

This is the name of the connection. We use the SAP naming convention `<SID>CLNT<CLIENT>` where `<SID>` is the system identifier—for example *SPR*—and `<CLIENT>` represents the client number, for example, *310*. In this case, the full name will be `SPRCLNT310`.

► **Connection type**

Here, you can select the connection type from the list we briefly described earlier. In this case, we are configuring a connection to another SAP application system and thus have to choose 3 R/3 CONNECTION.

► **Description**

Here, users can add comments. This is a required field that has to be filled with brief information about the connection.

After you enter these connection parameters and confirm them with the ⏎ key, the screen changes and displays specific fields for the SAP R/3 connection type (see Figure 1.3).

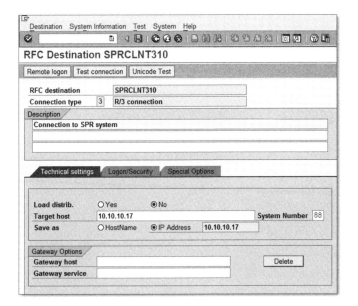

Figure 1.3 Transaction SM59—Example of R/3 Connection Details

You are now ready to specify the following remaining parameters:

▶ **Technical settings tab**
On the TECHNICAL SETTINGS tab, you have to provide the following information:

  ▷ **Target host**
  Here, you enter the IP or domain address of the partner's SAP server.

  ▷ **System number**
  This is a special number that identifies the SAP instance. It is necessary because several SAP instances can be installed on one server.

▶ **Logon/Security tab**
On the LOGON/SECURITY tab, you enter the USER NAME and PASSWORD of the communication user from the partner's system. The *communication user* is a special type of user who cannot log on to the SAP application system via an SAP logon.

You also have to specify the CLIENT NUMBER of the SAP application system with which you are trying to connect and the language used to exchange messages.

▶ **Special Options tab**

The SPECIAL OPTIONS tab contains the RFC TRACE functionality, which enables you to view—at a detailed level, byte by byte—all communication flowing through this connection. You can open the trace from the main view of Transaction SM59 and then analyze the communication. In Figure 1.4, you can see an example of a trace with an authorization error.

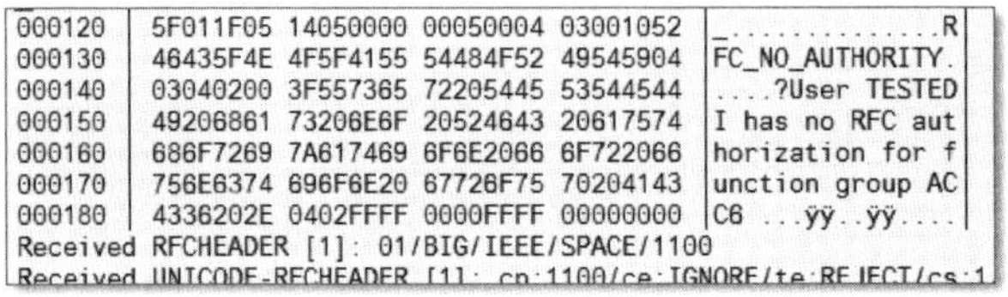

```
000120   5F011F05 14050000 00050004 03001052   |_............R|
000130   46435F4E 4F5F4155 54484F52 49545904   |FC_NO_AUTHORITY.|
000140   03040200 3F557365 72205445 53544544   |....?User TESTED|
000150   49206861 73206E6F 20524643 20617574   |I has no RFC aut|
000160   686F7269 7A617469 6F6E2066 6F722066   |horization for f|
000170   756E6374 696F6E20 67726F75 70204143   |unction group AC|
000180   4336202E 0402FFFF 0000FFFF 00000000   |C6 ...ÿÿ..ÿÿ....|
Received RFCHEADER [1]: 01/BIG/IEEE/SPACE/1100
Received UNICODE-RFCHEADER [1]: cp·1100/ce·IGNORE/te·REJECT/cs·1
```

Figure 1.4 Example of an RFC Trace

After entering all of the necessary data, you should test the connection by clicking on the TEST CONNECTION button. If the connection is working properly, you should see how fast the external system responds to your requests (see Figure 1.5).

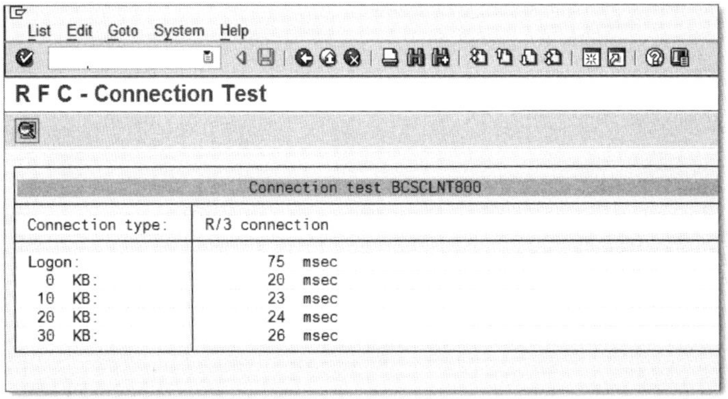

Figure 1.5 Results of Testing a Connection

If the external user is a dialog type—meaning that it can log on to the system using an *SAP Graphical User Interface* (SAP GUI)—another very helpful option exists. By clicking the REMOTE LOGON button, you can enter an external system via the standard SAP GUI. This is useful when normal network settings do not allow direct connections to the external system from outside the system landscape, as when firewall restrictions are in effect.

1.1.2 TCP/IP Type Connection

After the RFC destination of type R/3, the most commonly used type in IDoc integration scenarios is a TCP/IP connection. This is because it is a preferred way of accessing integration servers such as SAP Business Connector, as well as non-SAP applications.

The connection type TCP/IP CONNECTION (T) is technically a communication interface to external systems and programs by the *Remote Function Call Application Programming Interface* (RFC API). The RFC API is a set of C-language routines that perform certain communication tasks. Here is how to set up this type of connection:

1. To connect to an SAP Business Connector, aside from providing data common to all types of connections, you have to select the radio button REGISTERED SERVER PROGRAM.

2. Next, you need to enter a unique PROGRAM ID supplied to you by the partner that configured the other side of the connection. In our example, it is BXI_TO_ BCS_UNIQUE_PROGRAM_ID (see Figure 1.6).

Figure 1.6 Transaction SM59—Details of a TCP/IP Connection

The details of how to create a similar connection to SAP NetWeaver PI will be covered in Chapter 4.

After creating a physical connection to the partner's system via an RFC destination, you have to define the form for sending and receiving IDoc messages. In SAP systems, you have many options, all managed via Transaction WE21.

1.2   Port Definition

To understand the role of ports, take a look at Figure 1.7. Ports work as links from the application layers to the connections' physical layers. With transactional RFCs, which we will describe in the next section, the link leads to a previously defined connection in Transaction SM59. File ports link to physical destinations in the file system.

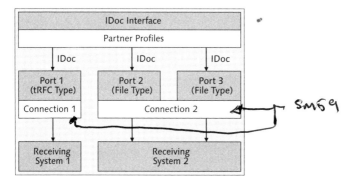

Figure 1.7 Port-to-Connection Relationships

Figure 1.8 shows the possible port types. After clicking one of them, you should see the existing ports. To add a new port, you have to place the cursor on a selected type and then click the NEW icon.

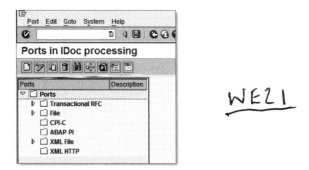

Figure 1.8 Transaction WE21—List of Possible Port Types

We will now show you how to define each of these port types. The most common is a *transactional RFC (tRFC) port*, which sends messages by invoking remote function calls at the external system. Special function modules are responsible for receiving such messages. This type is used in connecting SAP *Enterprise Resource Planning* (SAP ERP) to SAP NetWeaver PI, for example.

When sending and receiving IDocs using *R/3* or *TCP/IP* connections, you have to create at least one *tRFC port* for each connection. It will be used later on in partner profiles when you specify the technical receiver. Figure 1.9 shows an example of a tRFC port. The port's name is XI_00_010 and points to an RFC destination BXI that is defined in Transaction SM59.

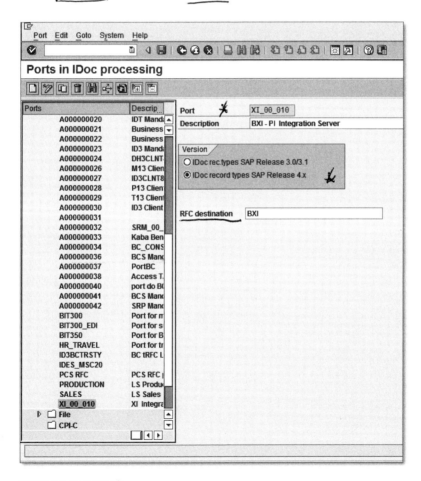

Figure 1.9 Port Details

Another commonly used type is a *file port*. In this case, messages will not be sent or received by an RFC destination but will instead be stored in the file system. When using a file port, the system writes a message to the file system and may also notify the receiving system via a synchronous RFC. This solution could be used instead of tRFC if large IDoc messages are used that could not be transferred via an RFC protocol.

IDocs transmitted to the file system via a file port can have two formats:

▶ **Flat files**

      ↳ FLAT or XML

Flat files have a simple structure. Each line represents one data segment. It consists of the segment's name and the segment's data. Figure 1.10 displays a portion of a flat-file IDoc of type INVOIC02.

```
 1  EDI_DC40  100000000000011607646C 3012  INVOIC02                                    INVOIC
 2  E2EDK01005        1000000000000116076000001000000001      EUR     1.00000      0001
 3  E2EDKA1003        10000000000001160760000020000000002RS                0000000027   Werk 0001
 4  E2EDKA1003        10000000000001160760000030000000002AG 0000000027                  TEST BS
 5  E2EDKA1003        10000000000001160760000040000000002RE 0000000027                  TEST BS
 6  E2EDKA1003        10000000000001160760000050000000002RG 0000000027                  TEST BS
 7  E2EDKA1003        10000000000001160760000060000000002BK               0001
 8  E2EDK02           1000000000000116076000007000000020090090000008                    20010725
 9  E2EDK02           1000000000000116076000008000000020014500000038
10  E2EDK02           1000000000000116076000009000000020020000000033                    20010725
11  E2EDK02           1000000000000116076000010000000020120080000011                    20010726
12  E2EDK02           1000000000000116076000011000000020170090000008
```

Figure 1.10 Example of a Flat-File IDoc

This format is difficult to read, which is why it is possible to generate documentation of the format. This can be sent to a partner to explain how to parse the data. Such *parser documents* can be generated from Transaction WE60.

After entering the IDoc type in the IDoc TYPE field of Transaction WE60, go to the menu DOCUMENTS and select CONTEXT PARSER. Figure 1.11 shows an example of a parser document for the INVOIC02 IDoc type. From the document, you are able to check the following:

▷ Segment names, description, hierarchy, and occurrence.

▷ Field names, description, type, length in bytes, and location in flat file data (start and end characters).

Figure 1.11 Parser Document for INVOICE02 IDoc

▶ **XML files**
In this mode, IDocs are written to disk as XML files. Segments and fields are converted to XML tags. You will find more information about this in Chapter 5.

1.3 Partner Profile Maintenance

You can think of partner profiles as connections between the technical system configuration—the connection and port described in Sections 1.1 and 1.2—and the business part of the configuration of outgoing and incoming IDocs. As for the latter, we will discuss in Chapter 2 how to configure *Message Control* (MC).

Partner profiles are collections of rules that tell the system how to process an IDoc message. For each IDoc type, whether inbound or outbound, there has to be a suitable registry because the same IDoc type could have different business meanings. For example, an ORDERS message type could represent a sales order or a purchase order. An IDoc of `INVOIC` message type could be entered in the SAP ERP component MM under logistics invoice verification, or entered directly into the Financials (FI) component.

[handwritten: PARTNER PROFILE USED TO DETERMIN IDOC USAGE AREA — MM or SD ETC FOR SAME IDOC. TYPE]

1.3.1 Parameters

To distinguish different business messages and to process them in different ways, each partner profile is set with the following parameters:

▸ **Partner type and partner number**

Partner type and partner number are connected. In the SAP system, IDocs could be addressed to different groups of partners represented as partner types. Here are the three most common types:

▹ **Customer**

In this case, partner numbers are retrieved from the customer table. All IDocs linked to sales and distribution processes can be addressed. Examples are outbound IDocs for order confirmations (message type `ORDRSP`), outgoing deliveries (`DELVRY`), sales invoices (`INVOIC`), and inbound IDocs such as purchase orders (`ORDERS`).

▹ **Vendor**

In this case, partner numbers are retrieved from a vendor table and used for IDocs connected with MM processes. With partner type `Vendor`, you can send IDocs with purchase orders (message type `ORDERS`), or receive inbound deliveries (`DELVRY`) or purchase invoices (`INVOIC`).

▹ **Logical system**

An alternative way is to use logical systems. A *logical system* is used to identify an individual client in a system. *Clients* in the SAP world are self-contained units in an SAP system with separate master records and their own sets of table entries. For example, one company could be represented as a single client when subsidiaries in different countries have their own clients on the same system.

Linking IDocs to a logical system is good practice if you are exchanging messages with groups of business partners. This way, you can create a single partner profile with a logical system name as a partner number, rather than having to create a separate partner profile for each of the business partners. The next section provides details on how to create a logical system.

▸ **Partner function**

Partner function is linked to partner type and identifies the function of the partner. In sales and distribution, business partners can play different roles, for example as sold-to party, ship-to party, or payer. This situation is similar to that in MM where, for example, a business partner can be used as an ordering party. This information can also be used to distinguish IDocs with the same message type sent to the same partner but used in different business contexts.

▸ **Message type**

Message type is a business type of IDocs, as was explained in detail at the beginning of this chapter.

▸ **Message code and message function**

Message code and message function are optional and in most cases used for grouping messages.

Logical systems are one of the most important IDocs receivers. In the next section we will show you how to create them.

1.3.2 Creating Logical Systems

A logical system has to be defined in the system before it can be used in a partner profile. Logical systems are managed in Transaction SALE or BD54.

1. To add a new logical system, use the following path: APPLICATION LINK ENABLING (ALE) • SENDING AND RECEIVING SYSTEMS • LOGICAL SYSTEMS.

2. You should see a list like the one shown in Figure 1.12. Enter a new entry or modify the existing entry and click the SAVE button.

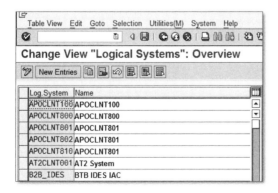

Figure 1.12 Transaction SALE—Example of a Logical Systems List

1.3.3 Customizing

Having explained the key fields used to distinguish IDocs, let us take a closer look at the parameters necessary to create partner profiles and how to customize them in the system.

IDoc partner profiles are maintained in Transaction WE20. From the standard SAP menu, you can reach this transaction via TOOLS • BUSINESS COMMUNICATION • IDOC BASIS • ADMINISTRATION • PARTNER PROFILES. The initial screen is shown in Figure 1.13. At the left side of screen, you will see a tree with different partner types. After you have clicked on one of them, the list of existing profiles for partner numbers should appear.

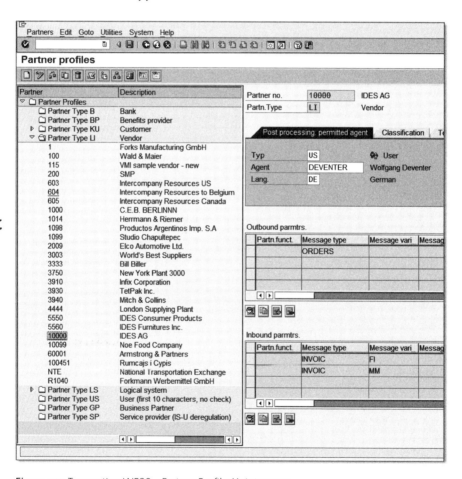

Figure 1.13 Transaction WE20—Partner Profile Maintenance

Each partner profile could have inbound and outbound IDoc messages attached to it. After selecting the partner number (from the tree at the left), you should see on the right side of screen two tables containing inbound and outbound messages.

The partner profile for the outbound IDoc message consists of several parameters, aside from those common for outbound and inbound messages:

▶ **Receiver port**
This parameter specifies how the IDocs are transferred to the external system. There are various technical options known as *port types*, described in Section 1.2.

▶ **Packet size**
The number of IDocs sent per RFC.

▶ **Transfer IDoc immediately/Collect IDocs**
This radio button lets you specify to send IDocs immediately or to store them in a database so they can be sent later. In the latter case, IDocs are sent by ABAP report `RSEOUT00`, which works as a scheduled job in the background.

▶ **Basic type**
The message type can be transmitted with different IDoc types, and you must choose one from a list available in the system. The type with the highest number is the latest version.

▶ **Application/Message type/Process code**
This functionality concerns Message Control. This is the mechanism for generating IDocs and other forms of output—such as printouts—during business transactions. This technology is described in Chapter 2.

Inbound IDocs also exist. The partner profile of the inbound section is a little different:

▶ **Process code**
Process code identifies the type of data processing for inbound processing. The IDoc interface uses the process code to find the business process that controls the conversion of the IDoc into the SAP application document. The business process can be a function module or a workflow event. In Chapter 2, we will describe process codes in more detail.

▶ **Trigger by background program/Trigger immediately**
For process codes that refer to function modules, you can indicate whether they have to be processed immediately or by a background job.

This section contained an introduction to partner profiles. A detailed, step-by-step guide is presented in Chapter 2.

1.4 Summary

This chapter provided you with information about the following:

- IDocs as containers for the exchange of data between SAP systems (and other systems).
- How to configure the transport layer for IDocs: connection to external systems and to ports (tRFC, flat files, and XML files).
- Partner profiles.

In the next chapter, we will show you how to configure SAP application systems for the automatic creation of IDoc messages during business transaction execution and how to process incoming IDocs.

2 Business Scenario Configuration

In this chapter, we will show you how to configure inbound and outbound IDocs with transactional data in different business scenarios. This book focuses only on the most common transactions from the SAP MM and SAP SD components. These two areas are strongly connected, and in real-life projects, IDocs sent from MM are often received in SD and vice-versa. A typical IDoc scenario configuration involves many steps. Some of these are common to all kinds of messages and some are not.

Because learning by example is much easier than learning by reading theory, we will reduce the amount of theory we cover to the minimum needed for understanding and use as many examples as possible.

There are several ways to create outbound IDocs. First, we will look at methods not covered by this book. In Figure 2.1, they are represented as a direct connection from applications (SAP transactions) to IDoc interfaces.

- **Manual creation**
  An application's ABAP code creates an IDoc and passes it to the interface via a special function module called `MASTER_IDOC_DISTRIBUTE`.

- **IDoc generation from BAPI**
  A *Business Application Programming Interface* (BAPI) is a set of function modules grouped by business functionalities. It is possible to generate a new IDoc type based on those function-module interfaces. You can run Transaction BAPI for details because each BAPI is well documented there.

In this book, however, we focus on *Message Control* (MC) and the *Shared Master Data tool*. The SMD tool is used for sending IDocs from master data. In Chapter 3, you will find a detailed description of how to configure SAP ERP for exchanging master data.

MC is a standard way of creating IDocs with business transaction data from the SD and MM components. The advantages of this method include its flexibility and the fact that it does not require any ABAP coding. The MC is a set of function modules that are invoked in the background by business transactions.

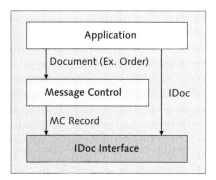

Figure 2.1 Flow of an Outbound IDoc

Let us take a look at the steps in the outbound IDoc flow presented in Figure 2.1. The procedure for IDoc creation using MC is as follows:

1. Applications invoke MC routines in the background to determine what to do with the document. By "application" we mean a group of SAP transactions that provides specific business functionality.

2. MC looks at a series of predefined conditions and—if the requirements are met—forwards the document to the IDoc interface.

3. The IDoc interface creates the proper IDoc and sends it to the receiving system using customized partner profiles, ports, and connections.

Figure 2.2 represents a common scenario between two companies using *Electronic Data Interchange* (EDI). In our model, we have a customer (BUYER ERP SYSTEM) and a vendor (VENDOR ERP SYSTEM).

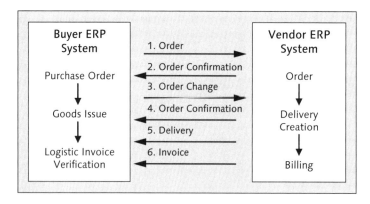

Figure 2.2 EDI Message Flow

The following actions take place:

1. The flow begins with creating a customer's purchase order. This step generates an EDI message, which creates a sales order in the vendor system.

2. Next, the vendor confirms the order and sends an acknowledgement (by IDoc) to the client.

3. The customer can then make changes and propagate them to the vendor system.

4. Next, the vendor confirms the changed order and sends an acknowledgement to the client.

5. This is followed by delivery creation, which generates a message to the customer. This message can be entered into the system as an inbound delivery. Because inbound delivery documents are very rare in real projects, we will only show you how to configure the outbound delivery from the vendor.

6. The process is completed by creating an invoice and sending it to the customer's system. The invoice is then entered in MM's logistics invoice-verification process.

Table 2.1 contains all of the messages we will use in our sample scenario.

IDoc type/ Message type	Description	Compo- nent	Time of creation	Action in the receiv- ing system
ORDERS05/ ORDERS	Purchase order	MM	While saving a new purchase order (ME21N)	Creates a new sales order.
ORDERS05/ ORDCHG	Purchase order change	MM	While saving the purchase order modification (ME22N)	Updates the sales order.
ORDERS05/ ORDRSP	Order confir- mation	SD	Sent after the cre- ation of a sales order and after each modification (VA02).	Updates certain pur- chase order details (e.g., confirmation lines, prices, etc.).

Table 2.1 List of IDoc Messages Used

IDoc type/ Message type	Description	Compo- nent	Time of creation	Action in the receiv- ing system
DELVRY03/ DESADV	Outbound delivery	SD	After creating the delivery or posting a goods issue (VL01N)	Creates an inbound delivery.
INVOIC02/ INVOIC	Sales invoice	SD	After posting a sales invoice (VF01)	Creates the MM and FI document for the purchase invoice and updates the purchase order history (logistic invoice verification).

Table 2.1 List of IDoc Messages Used (cont.)

Our examples are grouped by component. We will first present the configuration of inbound and outbound IDocs in MM, and then in SD, in the following order:

1. Sending outgoing purchase orders and changes (MM).
2. Sending delivery advice notes (MM).
3. Receiving incoming purchase invoices (MM).
4. Receiving sales orders and changes (SD).
5. Sending order confirmations (SD).
6. Sending sales invoices (SD).

The following sections will describe these examples in detail.

2.1   Purchase Orders and Purchase Order Changes in the MM Component

As the first example, we will use an electronic order exchange between a buyer and a supplier system (see Figure 2.3). In this case, the buyer creates a purchase order in the MM component (Transaction ME21N). After it has been saved, an IDoc is created and sent to the supplier system. On the receiver's side, the IDoc creates a sales order in the SD component, which you can view in Transaction VA03.

Transactions VA01, VA02, and VA03 are used to manage sales orders in the SAP application system.

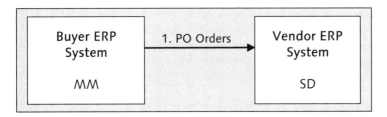

Figure 2.3 Order Flow

The configuration as presented will also allow sending changes. After making changes to the purchase order, the changes are automatically propagated to the sales order.

Let us take a look at the steps needed to configure the outgoing purchase order's IDoc message:

1. Select the appropriate application and procedure.
2. Create a new output type.
3. Define an access sequence or select an existing one.
4. Create a condition record.
5. Define a partner profile.
6. Fine-tune messages.
7. Enter the material number from the vendor's systems.
8. Test the scenario.

We will take a closer look at these steps in the next sections.

2.1.1   Selecting the Appropriate Application and Procedure

Selecting the appropriate application and procedure takes precedence in processing every MC. The *application code* is assigned to each application (group of SAP transactions) that uses MC for generating output messages. For example, "EF" is a code for purchasing and includes Transactions ME21N and ME22N, while "V1" is a code for sales, using Transactions VA01 and VA02. We will start the configuration of each message by selecting the appropriate application code.

1. First, take a look at the various applications and codes in Transaction NACE (see Figure 2.4). This is a complex tool for output configuration. Almost all steps are performed from this transaction.

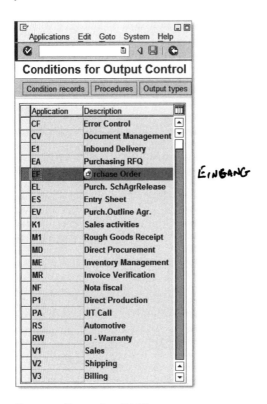

Figure 2.4 Transaction NACE

2. When configuring IDocs for purchase orders, we therefore have to select application EF (PURCHASE ORDER).

3. In the next screen, you can select a corresponding procedure (see Figure 2.5). Each application code contains a collection of *procedures*, which are connected to different kinds of business operations related to an application code. Examples of this would be purchase requisitions or purchase orders. The role of a procedure is to group output types that are connected with each business document type. Select procedure RMBEF1 on the right side and double-click the CONTROL label. You will see which output types are related to the procedure. In the next section, we will create a new output type and add it here.

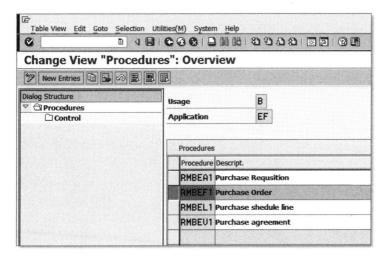

Figure 2.5 Transaction NACE—MC Procedures

2.1.2   Creating a New Output Type

The *output type* is a definition of a group of messages with the same business meaning. It represents various forms of output in the SAP system. Output types are used to assign parameters, for example how the output should be transmitted: by EDI, printouts, etc.

Now, let us return to our purchase-order configuration example. You have two options: You can use an existing output type or create a new one. For the example, you will select the second option. New output types can also be created with Transaction NACE. Proceed as follows:

1. Select the EF application that is responsible for MM purchasing and click the OUTPUT TYPES button.

2. The easiest way to add a new output type is by using a copy of an existing output type, remembering to stay in edit mode. For this operation, select the NEU *¥¥* output type (standard output for printouts and EDI), as shown in Figure 2.6.

3. Click the COPY icon on the standard bar at the top of screen. It looks like two yellow sheets of paper. Provide a new name, for example "ZSB", and access the output details by double-clicking the new output type's name (see Figure 2.7). Now that the new output type has been created, you can change parameters in relation to the original output.

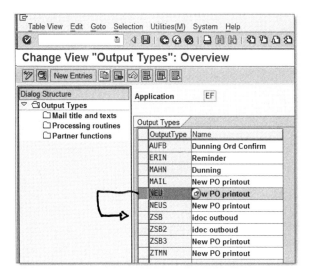

Figure 2.6 Copying an Existing Output Type

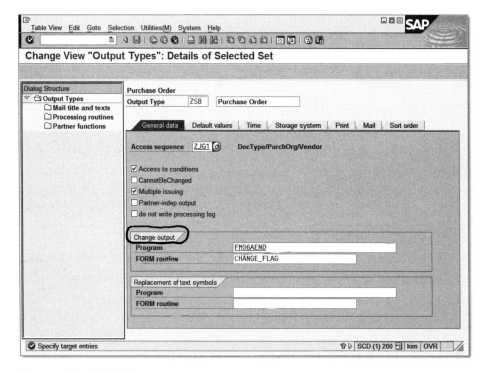

Figure 2.7 Details ZSB Output View

4. We will briefly describe each tab found in the detailed view of the new output type.

On the GENERAL DATA tab, you must select a proper ACCESS SEQUENCE. This is the most important setting to configure on this tab. We will discuss this in more detail in the next section when we show you how to set up the proper access sequence.

The other parameters on the screen (see Figure 2.7) are well documented; therefore, you can press F1 on each of them to obtain more information. For example, the checkbox ACCESS TO CONDITIONS indicates whether the system determines the output by searching for a valid condition record. If you leave it unchecked and if you are processing sales, shipping, or billing documents, the system automatically determines output from information stored in the customer master record. For our configuration, this option should be checked because we will base operations on condition records. These will be introduced in later sections.

You will use the output type you created to send a purchase order via an ORDERS message, but you also want to be able to notify the partner about changes in the purchase order. For example, you might need to add a new order item or change the ordered quantity. For this purpose, you will use the ORDCHG message. The relation between output type and suitable IDoc message type (such as ORDERS or ORDCHG) is configured in the partner profile. This also will be explained in subsequent sections.

The configuration for sending changes in documents is done in the CHANGE OUTPUT section (shown in Figure 2.7). This is where you insert your own ABAP programs, which determine whether you have a new document or a change in an existing document. For purchase orders, you can use the standard ABAP program prepared by SAP or create a new program with a definition of conditions that must be fulfilled to create a change message. The standard procedure for purchasing documents (orders and order changes) is contained in a program called FM06AEND and a form routine called CHANGE_FLAG. If you look into its source code, you will notice that it contains a procedure that checks whether the same type of output was generated before. If it was, the procedure sets the change flag to TRUE.

Now, access the DEFAULT VALUES tab (see Figure 2.8) and select 4 SEND IMMEDIATELY (WHEN SAVING THE APPLICATION) as DISPATCH TIME and 6 EDI as TRANSMISSION MEDIUM.

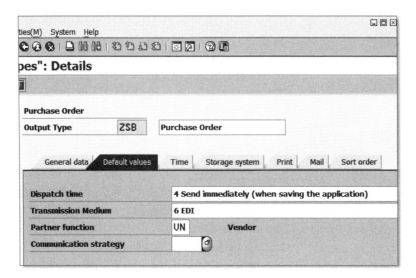

Figure 2.8 Default Values Tab for the ZSB Output

The most important parameter is the TRANSMISSION MEDIUM because it determines how the message will look. For example, the output could be an IDoc, printout, or email. Each output can have more than one transmission medium, and additional media can be set in the partner functions we will describe a little later.

The DISPATCH TIME is used to determine when the message has to be created. It could be created and sent immediately or saved in a queue and sent later.

Additional tabs are among the details of the output type: TIME, STORAGE SYSTEM, PRINT, MAIL, and SORT ORDER. For interface purposes, you do not have to customize all of them.

5. Next, take a look at the PARTNER FUNCTIONS section (see Figure 2.9). You will find it at the left side of the screen, in the tree below the OUTPUT TYPES folder.

6. You will see that we have added another option via the NEW ENTRIES button on the standard bar at the top of the screen: 6 EDI for the MEDIUM with the partner function LS (in the FUNCT column).

7. Partner functions are used to determine the control record of the IDoc and to set the configuration of the partner profile. We discussed different partner types in Chapter 1.

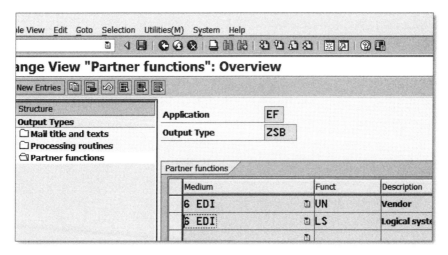

Figure 2.9 Partner Functions for the ZSB Output

Sending IDocs to the Logical System

In a partner profile, you can configure the settings for both outbound and inbound IDocs and also for logical systems. Adding the partner function LS to the output types (see Figure 2.9) allows you to enter the condition that will address the outgoing IDocs to the logical system.

Configuration of a logical system is appropriate when using an integration server such as SAP NetWeaver PI and many partners in EDI. For all of these partners, there will be only one partner profile because they are sent by a single port: a link to an RFC destination.

However, the existing partner function VN—derived from the original output type NEU we copied earlier—makes it possible to create IDocs addressed to a *vendor number* partner profile.

8. The last necessary setting in the EDI-enabled output type is a definition of processing routines. In generating IDocs, you have to specify the RSNASTED program (see Figure 2.10). This program creates an IDoc from business data and is always used for output types that are IDoc-enabled.

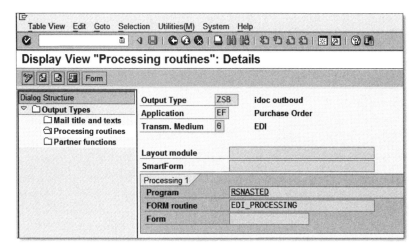

Figure 2.10 Processing Routines for the ZSB Output

With the settings described, you have created a new output type. You can now attach it to the proper procedure, as follows.

1. As described in the previous section, go to the main screen of Transaction NACE and select the EF application.

2. Next, select procedure RMBEF1 and double-click the CONTROL label (see Figure 2.5).

3. Now, click the NEW ENTRIES button and enter a number that has not yet been used in the STEP field, a "1" in the CNTR Field, and the output type name in the CTYPE field. In our case, this name is ZSB (see Figure 2.11).

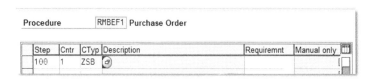

Figure 2.11 Adding an Output Type to a Procedure

4. After saving, this output type will be ready to be used with purchase order documents.

In the next sections, the output type will be attached to a condition record and will generate an IDoc.

2.1.3 Access Sequence

In the main screen of the output type (shown earlier in Figure 2.7), you have to specify the ACCESS SEQUENCE. The access sequence is very important because it contains a collection of business rules that are checked to decide whether to create a message. These business rules are stored in condition tables.

A *condition table* is a configurable definition of a group of keys. *Condition records* can be treated as an implementation of a condition table. In condition records, you enter real values such as a company code number or a purchase organization number. When documents are checked—for example, purchase orders—these values are compared with document values. If they are the same, the message defined by the output control is created. This message could be an IDoc or a printout, fax, email, and so on.

An example of a condition table for a purchase order could contain the following fields:

- Document type
- Purchase organization
- Vendor

An *access sequence* is a group of condition tables and determines the order in which the condition tables are searched during the creation of new messages. You can also define a procedure (EXCLUSIVE indicator) that specifies that if the search is successful, no further condition tables will be processed. For example, for purchase documents, the access sequence can have the values shown in Table 2.2.

Order number	Condition table fields	Exclusive indicator
1	Document type, Purchase organization, Vendor	True
2	Purchase organization, Vendor	True
3	Document type	False

Table 2.2 Example of an Access Sequence

You should always build access sequences in an order that puts the most sophisticated rules first, for the following reason: while you are entering condition records (filling them with real values), you can attach different media (EDI, printout, fax, etc.) to the same output type.

With that in mind, return to the already created OUTPUT TYPE ZSB (again, see Figure 2.7) and, from the drop-down list, select the appropriate ACCESS SEQUENCE for your business requirement. In our example, we have selected access sequence ZJG1 with the conditions shown in Figure 2.12. The access sequence contains three condition tables with the fields *Document type*, *Purchase organization*, and *Vendor number*.

2.1.4   Creating a Condition Record

At this point, you can specify real values (in condition tables) for previously defined conditions. From the business point of view, this is the most important part of your configuration. Here, you decide which IDoc documents should be sent to partners and when and where they should be sent. Proceed as follows:

1. The starting point for this operation is Transaction NACE. Select the EF (purchasing) application again and click the CONDITION RECORDS button.

2. A pop-up window with a list of output types opens; select the output type created in the previous section.

3. Next, the system reads the access sequence attached to the output type and presents the list of condition tables defined in this access sequence. You have to select one rule and click OK (see Figure 2.12).

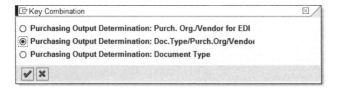

Figure 2.12 Possible Condition Tables for Condition Records

4. Because we have chosen Purchasing Output Determination: Doc.Type/ Purch.Org/Vendor as the condition table, we have to fill out the selection screen shown in Figure 2.13. For our example, we entered the following data:

 ▹ Purchasing Doc. Type: NB

 ▹ Purch. Organization: DZFI

 ▹ Vendor: 100003

However, you will have to enter different values based on your system configuration. That is, you will have to enter a purchasing document type, the purchase organization, and the vendor number from a range defined in your system.

Purchasing Doc. Type	NB		
Purch. Organization	DZFI		
Vendor	100003	⊘	to

Figure 2.13 First Step in Creating a Condition Record

5. In the next step, you have to enter what will be done with the document created for the selected values NB, DZFI, and 100003 (see Figure 2.14).

As a partner function (PartF), we selected VN. This means that the IDoc will be addressed to the vendor at the partner profile. We also decided that the output document will be an IDoc (value 6 in column M...) and will be sent immediately (value 4 in column Dat...).

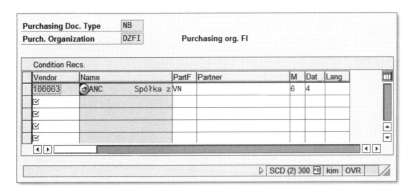

Figure 2.14 Second Step for Creating a Condition Record

In this section, you learned about access sequences and condition tables, which act like templates for items to be checked when generating an IDoc during document creation.

2.1.5   Defining a Partner Profile

With the configuration for sending purchase orders already done, and the technical details for sending IDocs entered, you now have to maintain the appropriate entries in the partner profile, as shown in Figure 2.15. Proceed as follows:

1. Open Transaction WE20 and add a partner number that will be the receiver of order messages. The vendor type is represented by the LI abbreviation (PARTNER TYPE LI).

2. In our example, we have chosen vendor 100003, but you can enter any vendor number defined in your system that you entered in the condition record.

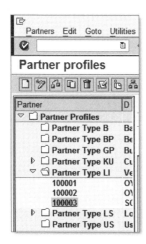

Figure 2.15 Transaction WE20—Vendor Partners in Partner Profiles

3. The next step is adding a definition of outgoing messages. For the purchase order and purchase order change in the example scenario, you have to add the message types ORDERS and ORDRCHG.

4. Click the ADD icon belonging to outgoing messages (in the middle of the screen), and specify the details provided in Table 2.3.

Basic Information	
Partn.function	VN (Vendor)
Message type	ORDERS
Outbound Options tab	
Receiver port	Press F4, and select the port you created earlier (for example, in Chapter 1, you created a port named XI_00_010). The port is a link to a technical connection to another system.
Output mode	Transfer IDoc immed.
Basic type	ORDERS05
Message Control tab	
Application	EF
Message type	ZSB (the name of the message type that was created previously and that is used in the condition record)
Process code	ME10
Change message	NO

Table 2.3 Partner Profile Settings for Purchase Orders

5. The second message is for the change order process. The definition of the partner profile is very similar to that of the ORDER message (see Table 2.4).

Basic Information	
Partn.function	VN (Vendor)
Message type	ORDCHG
Outbound Options tab	
Receiver port	Press F4, and select the port you created previously. Remember: The port is a link to a technical connection to another system.
Output mode	Transfer IDoc immed.
Basic type	ORDERS05

Table 2.4 Partner Profile Settings for Purchase Order Changes

Basic Information	
Message Control tab	
Application	EF
Message type	ZSB (the name of the message type created previously and used in the condition record)
Process code	ME11
Change message	YES

Table 2.4 Partner Profile Settings for Purchase Order Changes (cont.)

In Figure 2.16, you will see a screen shot of the MESSAGE CONTROL tab of the ORD-CHG partner profile. This is simply a link to the MC and the condition technique described earlier.

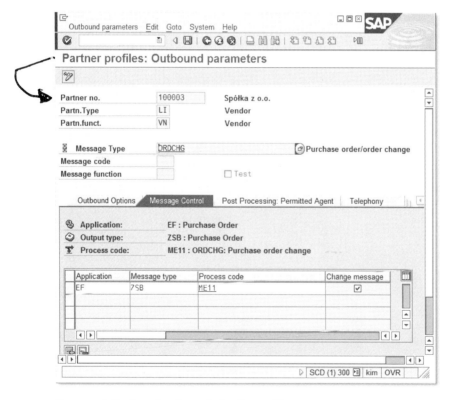

Figure 2.16 Configuration for an Order Change Message

Process Codes

The PROCESS CODE on the MESSAGE CONTROL tab defines how the system creates the message. In this case, the process code ME10 is connected with the function module IDOC_ OUTPUT_ORDERS, which creates an IDoc from purchase order data.

Process codes are used with outgoing and incoming IDocs. They are defined in special transactions. You can find them by navigating to TOOLS • BUSINESS COMMUNICATION • IDOC BASIS • DEVELOPMENT and then OUTBOUND PROCESSING SETTINGS/MC (Transaction WE41) and INBOUND PROCESSING SETTINGS (Transaction WE42) in the SAP menu.

After you have entered these parameters, the list of outgoing IDocs in the main screen of partner profile (Transaction WE20) should look like the one shown in Figure 2.17.

Outbound parmtrs.

	Partn.funct.	Message type	Message vari	MessageFun	Test
	VN	ORDCHG			☐
	VN	ORDERS			☐

Figure 2.17 Transaction WE20—Outbound Parameters for Purchase Orders

Partner profiles describe the technical part of the configuration: They show which IDoc type will be chosen, how it should be filled with data—as indicated by the message code—and where the IDocs have to be sent technically, as indicated by the port. The link to the MC is made by entering the output type.

2.1.6 Fine-Tuning Messages

For IDoc configuration for purchase orders, you have to complete one more activity: selecting which messages will be used by the purchasing process. To customize these settings, proceed as follows:

1. Start Transaction SPRO.

2. Select SAP REFERENCE IMG • MATERIAL MANAGEMENT • PURCHASING • MESSAGES • OUTPUT CONTROL • MESSAGE TYPES • DEFINE MESSAGE TYPES FOR PURCHASE ORDER • FINE-TUNED MESSAGE CONTROL.

3. Add two new items (via the NEW ENTRIES button):

▷ Operation 1—creation of the message—for created type ZSB

▷ Operation 2—changing the message—for created type ZSB

These steps are shown in Figure 2.18.

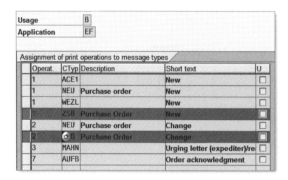

Usage	B			
Application	EF			

Assignment of print operations to message types

Operat.	CTyp	Description	Short text	U
1	ACE1		New	☐
1	NEU	Purchase order	New	☐
1	WEZL		New	☐
1	ZSB	Purchase Order	New	☑
2	NEU	Purchase order	Change	☐
2	SB	Purchase Order	Change	☐
3	MAHN		Urging letter (expediter)/re	☐
7	AUFB		Order acknowledgment	☐

Figure 2.18 Fine-Tuning of Purchasing Messages

You have now completed the customizing process for sending purchase orders via IDoc.

2.1.7 Entering the Material Numbers from the Vendor's Systems

The following setting is optional and is not directly related to EDI configuration. Nevertheless, it is helpful for entering orders in an external system because it has its own master data inside the IDoc document.

By creating a *material info record*, you can assign external material numbers from a partner's system for your materials. The external material numbers are then placed inside outbound IDocs in segment E1EDP19, with the qualifier 002.

Material info records are maintained in Transactions ME11, ME12, and ME13.

1. To enter an external number for a material, run Transaction ME11, and enter both the vendor and the material number in the appropriate fields.

2. On the next screen (see Figure 2.19), fill the field VENDOR MAT. NO. in the VENDOR DATA section. This is the place for the number from the vendor system.

Setting the vendor material number causes the vendor system to operate on the basis of its own master data.

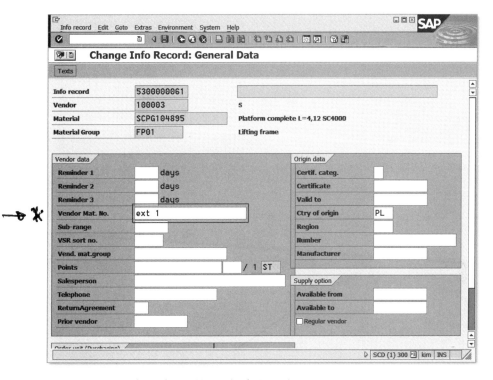

Figure 2.19 External Number in Material Info Record

2.1.8 Testing the Scenario

After completing all of these steps, you are ready for a first test of our scenario.

1. Run Transaction ME21N, and create a new purchase order by filling all required fields, as follows:

   ▸ **Vendor number**
   Select the vender number from the condition record.

   ▸ **Purchase organization**
   Select the purchase organization available in your system.

   ▸ **Purchase group**
   Select the purchase group available in your system.

   ▸ **Company code**
   To fill this field, you have to display the ORG. DATA tab, as shown in Figure 2.20. Every field you need to fill has an F4 help to select a value from a list.

You can now add a new item (see Figure 2.20):

▸ **Material number**
You can also use F4 help and select any material from the list.

▸ **Quantity**
For example, enter one piece.

▸ **Plant**
Select the plant that is available in your system.

If you have any problems with filling the required fields, Figure 2.20 shows an example from a test system.

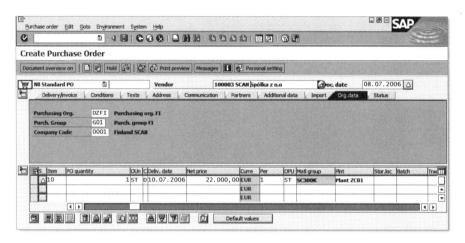

Figure 2.20 Transaction ME21N—Creating a Purchase Order

2. When all of the necessary fields are filled, click the MESSAGES button at the top of the screen. You can see the proposed output in Figure 2.21. This is the output proposed by MC and shows its configuration at work. The system reads a condition table, compares it with the purchase order data, and creates an output. In our case, NEU will be a printout and ZSB will generate an IDoc after saving the document.

3. Save your order (by clicking the SAVE icon) and run Transaction WE02, the IDoc list.

4. Accept default data at the selection screen, and check that a new outbound IDoc was created. If you have any problems, refer to Chapter 4 where this transac-

tion is described in detail. Finally, you should have an IDoc that looks like the one shown in Figure 2.22.

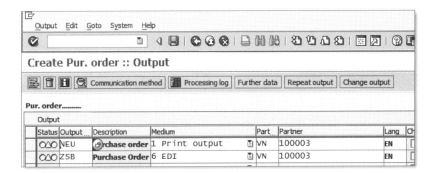

Figure 2.21 Messages Assigned to a Purchase Order

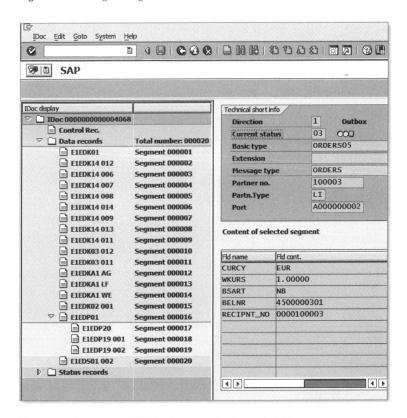

Figure 2.22 Transaction WE02—Preview of a Generated IDoc

By reading this section, you have become familiar with the complex configuration for sending IDocs. This example showed you how to configure purchase orders; the configuration for other business documents is very similar, as you will see in subsequent sections.

2.2 Receiving Purchase Order Confirmations

In our scenario, after a purchase order is sent from the MM component, it is received by the SD component, and from this order, a sales order is created (this configuration is described in Section 2.4). The order is then confirmed by the vendor (see Section 2.5). Staying within the MM component, we will show you how to configure the system for receiving these confirmations.

For the next phase of our business scenario, we will assume that our partner has received our purchase order, saved it in its system, and now sends an order confirmation (see Figure 2.23). For this purpose, a special message type is used called *orders IDoc*, or ORDRSP (order response).

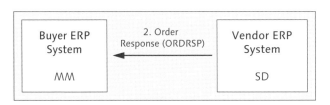

Figure 2.23 Order Confirmation Flow

To configure automatic creation of an order confirmation, you have to perform the following steps:

1. Creating an appropriate partner profile.
2. Configuring confirmation control in Customizing for purchasing. This is MM Customizing for inserting confirmations with schedule lines to an order's positions.
3. Configuring the confirmation keys in material infotypes.
4. Testing the new settings.

These steps will be described in the next sections.

2.2.1 Creating an Appropriate Partner Profile

We will assume that the order confirmation comes to us from logical system SCDCLNT300. If this is the first message from that system, you have to add this system to your system's Customizing (described in Chapter 1). Proceed as follows:

1. Run Transaction WE20 to create an appropriate partner profile.

2. Place the cursor at PARTNER TYPE LS and click the NEW icon (the blank sheet icon). Enter the name "SCDCLNT300" into the PARTNER NO. field, and click SAVE.

   If the name of the logical system is not accepted, you have to add it by using Transaction SALE.

3. You are now able to add a new incoming message. Click the '+' icon below the INCOMING PARAMETERS table and enter the data from Table 2.5.

Parameter name	Value
Message type	ORDRSP
Process code	ORDR
Processing by function module	Trigger immediate

Table 2.5 Inbound Partner Profile for ORDRSP IDoc

2.2.2 Setting Up Confirmation Control in Customizing for Purchasing

If you want to know about potential changes in an order—such as a change of quantity or delivery date—you have to maintain confirmation control for MM purchasing. Proceed as follows:

1. Run Transaction SPRO.

2. From the Customizing tree, select MATERIALS MANAGEMENT • PURCHASING • CONFIRMATION • SET UP THE CONFIRMATION CONTROL.

3. The details are shown in Figure 2.24. In this book, we do not explain all of the details connected with this functionality because this is strictly an MM Customizing issue.

4. For entering an EDI order response, use the confirmation key 0001. Select CONFIRMATION SEQUENCE on the left side of the screen (see Figure 2.25).

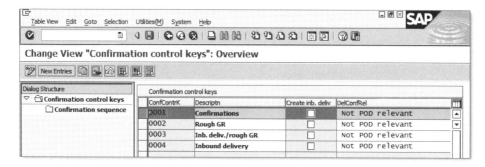

Figure 2.24 Transaction SPRO — Confirmation Controls

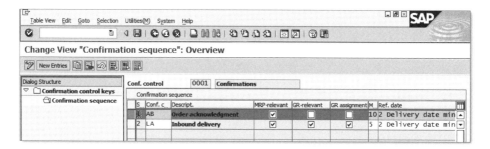

Figure 2.25 Transaction SPRO — Confirmation Sequence of Control Key 0001

Field	Example value	Description
Monitoring	10	Value in days that specifies how soon a confirmation must be received
Ref date	Purchase order date plus monitoring time or delivery date minus monitoring time	Reference date for the vendor confirmation-monitoring period
TolTooEarl	999	Tolerance in days for too-early confirmation of delivery dates via EDI (error)
TolTooLate	999	Tolerance in days for too-late confirmation of delivery dates via EDI (error)
Price	Yes or No	Adopt price change (inbound EDI only).

Table 2.6 List of EDI-Relevant Fields for the Confirmation Sequence

Field	Example value	Description
Pr. ov. %	50 %	Permitted price overrun in % (inbound EDI only)
Pr. ov. %	50 %	Permitted price shortfall in % (inbound EDI only)

Table 2.6 List of EDI-Relevant Fields for the Confirmation Sequence (cont.)

5. The first item in the list has configuration category AB. This type of confirmation will be created from an IDoc. Here, referring to Table 2.6, you can set how the system should react after receiving this type of IDoc.

2.2.3 Setting Up Confirmation Keys in Material Infotypes

The last configuration task for receiving order confirmations is setting up the confirmation keys in the material infotypes.

To do so, you have to determine exactly which confirmation keys have to be created for the vendor, material, and purchase organization. For this setting, you will again use the material info records. Proceed as follows:

1. Run Transaction ME11 and fill in the required data. In this case, this is the vendor number, material number, and purchase organization.

2. Click the PURCH ORG. DATA 1 button, and enter "0001" for the CONFCONTRK (confirmation key) parameter (see Figure 2.26). It displays the configuration key that was customized in the previous section.

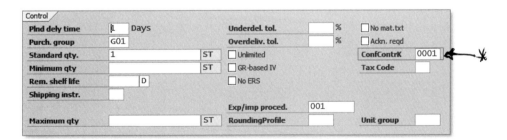

Figure 2.26 List of EDI-Relevant Fields for the Confirmation Sequence

After customizing the confirmation control, you are ready to run some tests. You will do this in the next section.

2.2.4 Testing the New Settings

To test whether the purchase order confirmation was received correctly, do the following:

1. Create a new purchase order using Transaction ME21N, as explained previously. Send it to your partner.

2. In Transaction WE02, first check whether an ORDERS IDoc was sent. After a while, check whether the new IDoc (ORDRSP) was received. If it arrives and has a green status (see Chapter 3 for details), the order should be confirmed.

3. Run Transaction ME23N, and select the CONFIRMATIONS tab at the ITEM level. In Figure 2.27, you can see that the vendor has confirmed two items of ordered material on April 28, 2006. From the upper table you can see that you ordered three items, and that the vendor reduced the order quantity to two items.

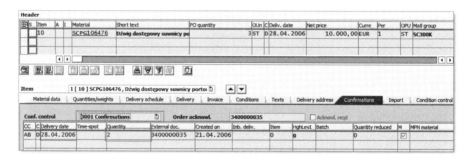

Figure 2.27 Transaction ME23N—Confirmation of Purchase Order Item

These steps allow you to receive inbound order confirmations. We will now look at the next document, which also refers to the purchase order: the incoming invoice.

2.3 Logistic Invoice Verification

Our sample process ends by receiving an invoice from the vendor (see Figure 2.28). In the sales and distribution processes, the partner often creates the outbound delivery at his system before invoicing takes place. This step could generate an IDoc message, which can be entered as an inbound delivery to the MM component. Because the inbound delivery document is very rare in real projects, we will skip this step and move on to receiving incoming invoices.

Electronic invoices arrive via the INVOIC IDoc.

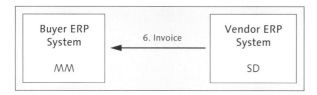

Figure 2.28 Invoicing Process Flow

In the SAP application system, you can create these kinds of documents in two ways: The first is to enter them directly to financial accounting; the second is called *logistic invoice verification*.

Because invoices in our process are connected to purchase orders, we will select the second option for the following example. The system configuration will involve the following:

1. Creating the appropriate partner profiles.
2. Allocating the company code, tax code mapping, and "special program parameters."
3. Testing the new settings.

The next sections will explain these steps in detail.

2.3.1 Creating Appropriate Partner Profiles

To create the appropriate partner profiles, you need to do the following:

1. Enter Transaction WE20.
2. We will assume that invoices come from logical system SCDCLNT300. You have already added this logical system during the configuration of order confirmations.
3. Select the logical system in the tree at the left side of the screen, and click the ADD icon below the INCOMING PARAMETERS table. Here, you have to enter the values from Table 2.7. These values will cause that system to run the function module attached to process code INVL if an INVOIC message with message code MM arrives.

Parameter name	Value
Message type	INVOIC
Message code	MM
Process code	INVL
Processing by function module	Trigger immediately

Table 2.7 Inbound Partner Profile for INVOIC

At the beginning of this section, we mentioned entering invoices directly into financial accounting. In this case, the partner profile will be similar but you will have to select process code INVF and regular message code FI.

The next step does not apply to IDocs in general but is specific to our scenario.

2.3.2 Allocating Company Code, Tax Code Mapping, and "Special Program Parameters"

You now have to make further adjustments, as follows:

1. Enter Transaction SPRO and select MATERIAL MANAGEMENT • LOGISTIC INVOICE VERIFICATION • EDI (see Figure 2.29). Here, you have three entries for customizing incoming EDI invoices.

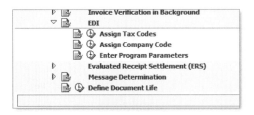

Figure 2.29 Transaction SPRO—Relevant Tasks for EDI Logistic Invoice Verification

2. The first is the tax-code mapping. The system that has created the invoice can have a different tax code, or the invoice could have been created in a different country. In this case, you have to enter an appropriate mapping in the ASSIGN TAX CODES program. To run the program, double-click the name.

3. The mapping will be created for the sender of the IDoc, just as in the partner profile. You have to enter the PARTNER TYPE (in our case, it will be LS for "logical

the agent type responsible for handling of errors .

For every message send to the partner we have a outbound record and for evry message coming from the partner we have the inbound record . We specify the message in the otbound/inbound records ,double clicking will take us to the detailed screen where the IDOC Type ,Port and whether the IDCO will be immediatelt processed or collected are mentioned.

http://sap.niraj.tripod.com

Add To Favorite	http://sap.niraj.tripod.com
Google Search	SAP ABAP Bdc Code

(●) Search http://sap.niraj.tripod.com ( ) Search www

Recommend
This Site

BDC Code UserExits & Enhancements SAPScript Explained SAPScript Graphics
SAPScript Print Program ABAP ListViewer ABAP Code Best Of SAP ABAP Links
My Resume Contact Information Free Website Submission Free Domain Search
Free HoroScope Submit Your Code Add URL SAP Forum Adverise With Us
Dialog Programming SAP Books Dialog Programming HOME

http://sap.niraj.tripod.com   **Niraj Visnoi *INDIA * niraj_visnoi@consultant.com**
CELL No. 91 9911413767

processing status can be seen in detail.

BD10 Material Master Data Distribution .
Based on Message MATMAS.

BD12 Customer Master Data Distribution .
Based on Message CREMAS.

BD14 Vendor Master Data Distribution
Based on Message DEBMAS .

BDFG Generate ALE Interface for BAPI.
Here we specify the Business Object and the BAPI Function module for which the interface has to be created.

WE31 Segment Editor.
This is used to create segments. We create the segment type and segment definition is automatically created by editor e.g. Z1DUMMY is segment type and Z2DUMMY is the segment definition. We specify the fields and the data elements these cp\orresponds to create segments.

WE30 IDOC Editor
It is used to create a new IDOC Type or IDOC Extension .We specify the segments that will be addd to the IDOC type.

WE02/05 IDOC List.
Various selct options and parameters are provided to select IDOCs depending on the date, direction , mesage type etc.

WE20 Partner Profile
Here we create partner profile for each and every partner from / to which
the messeges will be exchanged. There are 6 types of DT owner the ch

system"), the PARTNER NUMBER (in our case, SCDCLNT300), the TAX TYPE and TAX RATE from the sender's system, and the equivalent tax code (Tx) from your system. This procedure has to be repeated for each tax code from the sender's system (see Figure 2.30). We left the field CTY (City) blank because it is not used. After the configuration is completed, click SAVE and return to the SPRO menu.

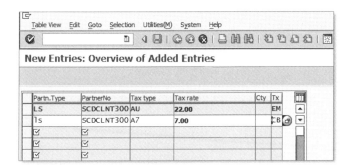

Figure 2.30 Example Tax Code Mappings

4. Next, you need to tell the system in which company code the invoice should be inserted. More than one company subsidiary can work on the same system and because an invoice is a financial document, you have to specify where it should be posted. Run the ASSIGN COMPANY CODE program from the SPRO menu (via double-click), re-enter the sender of the IDoc (as you did in the previous step), and then insert the appropriate company code. In our test case, we specified 0001 (see Figure 2.31) but you will have to specify your own company code. Use F4 help for a list of company codes.

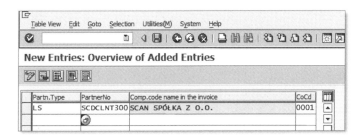

Figure 2.31 Example of Company Code Assignment

5. The last step allows you to enter the document type for the invoice and specify how it will be processed: automatically or parked while the document awaits

approval. To do so, run ENTER PROGRAM PARAMETERS. In the details, enter the sender data (PARTNER TYPE and PARTNER NUMBER, as in the previous steps) and a company code via double-clicking.

6. You also have to fill the field INVOICE DOC. TYPE (see Figure 2.32) because it determines the type of document that will be created from the IDoc. The invoice type plays a role in accounting (FI component). You can ask your MM key user or business process owner which invoice type should be created from the IDoc. In our test case, we have selected the ZM type, but your actual choice depends on your individual system configuration.

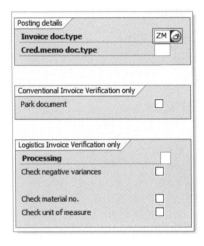

Figure 2.32 Program Parameters for an EDI Invoice

By filling in the data in these three SPRO settings and creating a partner profile, you have finished configuring the system for incoming invoices via IDoc. In the next section, we will show you how to test these settings.

2.3.3 Testing the New Settings

To test your new settings, ask your partner to send an invoice for a previous order (or do it by yourself after reading Section 2.7), and wait for the IDoc. Check whether it enters the system with a green status. Next, open the purchase order (Transaction ME23N) and look at the PURCHASE ORDER HISTORY tab at the ITEM level (see Figure 2.33). Clicking the document number will cause the invoice to display (see Figure 2.34).

Figure 2.33 Example of Viewing an Invoice Connected with a Purchase Order

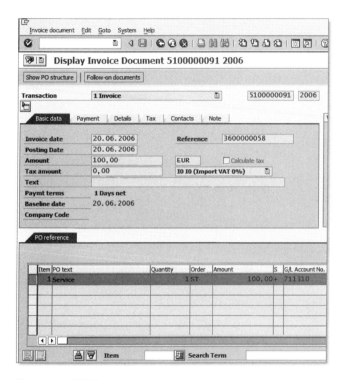

Figure 2.34 MM Invoice

The incoming purchase invoice was the last type of message from the MM scenarios. Next, you will learn how to send and receive SD documents by using IDocs.

2.4 Processing Inbound Orders in SD

Out first example from the SD component will be an incoming purchase order via IDoc.

We will assume that our partner sends us MM purchase orders (see Section 2.1), and we have to configure the system for automatic creation of a sales order from a purchase order. As you know, purchase orders are represented as ORDERS IDoc messages. The vendor has to be ready for order changes represented by the ORD-CHG type.

The business process (see Figure 2.35) is exactly the same as in Section 2.1, but now we will prepare the system to receive messages.

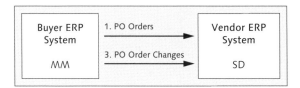

Figure 2.35 Order Flow

As in the previous cases, the first thing to do is establish a connection to a partner system via Transaction SM59 and then create an appropriate port via Transaction WE21. Subsequent actions are as follows:

1. Creating suitable partner profiles with inbound parameters.

2. Converting external partner numbers.

3. Assigning a customer to SD organizational data.

These steps will be explained in the next sections.

2.4.1 Creating Suitable Partner Profiles with Inbound Parameters

We will again start by creating partner profiles. As in the previous examples, you have to know the sender's name to configure the inbound messages. Proceed as follows:

1. If you have sample IDocs from your partner, you can take a look inside a control record via Transaction WE02 (see Figure 2.36). In this example, a partner profile should be created for the logical system (LS) SCDCLNT300 (buyer system). If you do not have any sample IDocs, try to implement the configuration from Section 2.1 and send the IDocs to the same system.

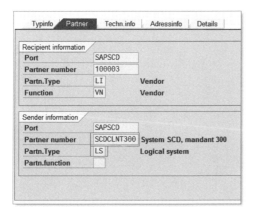

Figure 2.36 IDoc Control Record

2. Run Transaction WE20, and look for this logical system profile; if it does not exist, add the value from PARTNER NUMBER to the appropriate PARTNER TYPE. In this case, this is SCDCLNT300, located below PARTNER TYPE LS (see Figure 2.37).

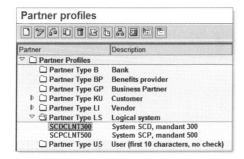

Figure 2.37 Transaction WE20—Partner Profile

3. Next, you have to specify the detailed information concerning the ORDERS and ORDCHG messages.

   ▷ Regarding the ORDERS message type for incoming messages, the set of required parameters is smaller. Most important are the MESSAGE TYPE (without a message version) and the PROCESS CODE (the description how the message will be processed). For sales order creation, use the ORDE process code. From a technical point of view, this process code executes the IDOC_INPUT_ORDERS function module. This module is based on batch-input technology, and users can easily debug these types of orders. This issue will be described at the end of this section.

▷ The sales order changes are made using MESSAGE TYPE ORDCHG and PROCESS CODE ORDC (see Figure 2.38).

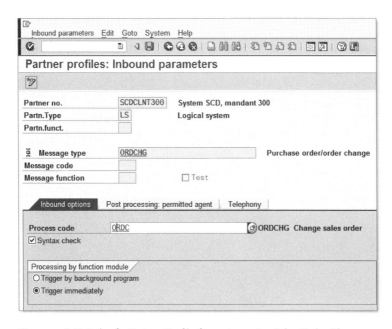

Figure 2.38 Details of a Partner Profile for an Incoming Sales Order Change

Customizing done in these two steps prepares the system to receive orders from your partner. You now have to tailor IDoc messages to your master data (partner numbers) by completing two more steps.

2.4.2 Converting External Partner Numbers

After you have configured partner profiles for ORDERS and ORDCHG, the system is ready for entering sales orders. But if the messages' data is not tailored to a specific system's master data, IDocs will be inserted with errors.

These errors can be caused by problems such as wrong master data for the partner numbers. To handle this, special utilities exist in Transaction SPRO. You can reach them via the following path: SPRO • SALES AND DISTRIBUTION • ELECTRONIC DATA INTERCHANGE • EDI MESSAGES • CONFIGURE EDI PARTNERS (see Figure 2.39).

Figure 2.39 Tools for EDI-SD Configuration

First, we will run the tool CONVERT EXTERNAL TO INTERNAL PARTNER NUMBERS. IDocs are created in external systems, and the partner numbers also originate there. Often, these numbers are different and refer to different customers, or to non-existent customers. You have to convert them to your master data. If you have problems, press [F1] to see the field's description before entering any data.

This step allows you to map an external partner's numbers to the corresponding data in the receiving system.

2.4.3 Assigning a Customer to SD Organizational Data

Sales orders are created in an environment described by SD organizational data such as sales organization, distribution channel, and division (these three are mandatory) and also an order type. There are two ways to create a proper order via IDoc:

▶ The first way is to receive all organization data in an IDoc message. Take a look inside a message using Transaction WE02 (described in Chapter 4). Organizational data and order type are stored in the E1EDK14 segment (*Document Header Organizational Data*). You can find it by using the ORGID field preceded by a suitable qualifier. You can find the list of qualifiers for this segment in Table 2.8.

Qualifier	Meaning
012	Order type
007	Distribution channel
008	Sales organization
006	Division

Table 2.8 SD Organizational Data at Segment E1EDK14

▶ The second method, used when these fields are not available in the IDoc, is the tool Assign Customer/Vendor to Sales Organization Data. The path to the tool is analogous to the partner number conversion, shown in Figure 2.39.

In this tool, you have to enter the customer number (this is a number from your SAP system) and then the number under which you are managed as a vendor in the customer's system. These two fields are treated as the key for SD organization data determination. As a result, you can now enter fields, sales organization, distribution channel, division, and sales order type that you want to see in orders created for specified customers. The screenshot for this operation is shown in Figure 2.40.

Customer	Vendor number	SOrg.	SOrg description	DChl	DChannel descrip.	Dv	Division descrip.	SaTy	SD type descrip.
112	00000115	1000	Germany Frankfu	10	Final customer sale	00	Cross-division		
112	115	1000	Germany Frankfu	10	Final customer sale	00	Cross-division		
1110	0000001014	1020	Germany Berlin	22	Industrial customer	00	Cross-division		
3070		3020	USA Denver	12	Sold for resale	00	Cross-division	OR	Standard Ord
3070	0000003070	3020	USA Denver	12	Sold for resale	00	Cross-division	OR	Standard Ord
3580	5580	3020	USA Denver	30	Internet Sales	00	Cross-division		
30099	0000010099	3000	USA Philadelphi	01	Direct Sales	05	Foods		
30099	NOEFOODS	0002		01	Direct Sales	05	Foods		

Figure 2.40 EDSDC Table Determination of Sales Area

At this point, you have completed the customizing needed to determine the master SD data if this data is missing in the IDoc message and configuration for inbound orders is done. Ask your partner to send an order, and test your settings by opening Transaction WE02 and looking for incoming IDoc statuses.

2.4.4   Testing and Debugging Incoming IDoc Sales Orders

Finally, we will share an easy way to debug incoming IDocs and look for errors. The function module, which is used to create a sales order from an IDoc, makes use of a batch input technique. Therefore, you can view, one by one, all of the screens of Transaction VA01 and see how they are being filled with the data coming from an IDoc. Proceed as follows:

1. To debug, run Transaction WE19 (test tool for IDoc processing), and enter the appropriate IDoc number, which can be found in Transaction WE02.

2. Click the Inbound function module button, and enter the name of the function module (`IDOC_INPUT_ORDERS`). It is very important that you select In foreground (see Figure 2.41). If this checkbox is not checked, the IDoc will process in the background and you will not see the corresponding screens filled with data from the IDoc.

3. Pressing ⏎ after the execution will move you to the next screen of Transaction VA01.

4. In case of errors, you can also manually change IDocs, process them, and inform your partner what should be changed for proper processing.

In this section, we have explained how to create an order from an incoming IDoc. In the next section, we will show you how to send an order confirmation.

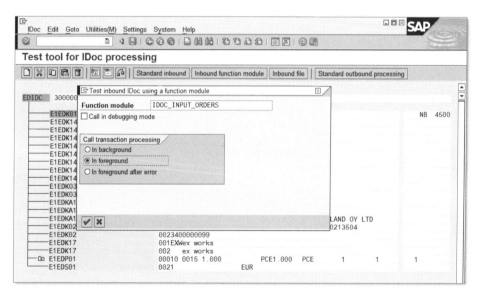

Figure 2.41 Test Tool for Processing IDocs

2.5   Outbound Order Confirmation

After receiving an order via an IDoc, a confirmation should be sent saying that the sales order was created and that the vendor is preparing the delivery (see Figure 2.42).

It is also possible at this point to change information such as the delivery date or remove an item that the vendor is not able to realize and inform a partner about it. In this case, you use the ORDRSP (order response) message. Our configuration will cause every saved change in a sales order to generate an ORDRSP IDoc.

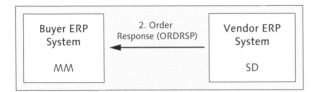

Figure 2.42 Order Confirmation Flow

As with the other outgoing IDoc configuration, you have to complete the following steps:

1. Selecting or creating a new output type.

2. Selecting an appropriate procedure.

3. Creating entries in condition record tables.

4. Configuring the partner profile.

2.5.1 Selecting or Creating a New Output Type

You will find the configuration options for sales orders in the V1 (Sales) application of Transaction NACE. In the following steps, we are exploring possible output types:

1. Run Transaction NACE, select the V1 application from the list, and click the OUTPUT TYPES button.

2. In the DIALOG STRUCTURE on the left side, click OUTPUT TYPES. The result should look like what you see in Figure 2.43.

3. Select BA01 EDI ORDER RESPONSE, and check whether it is ready for EDI. To do so, check the details in Table 2.9.

4. With these values, the output has everything needed for EDI processing. A good way to change details—such as the access sequence—is to create a copy of the output type and then enter your own data. For our purposes, we will maintain the original version of this output.

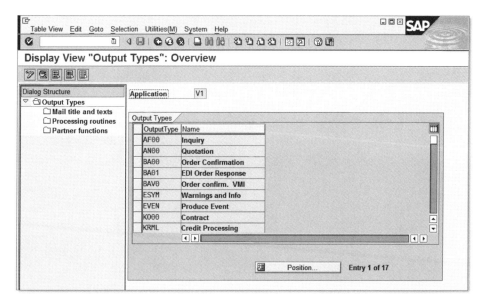

Figure 2.43 Output Types for Application V1 (Sales)

General data tab	
Access sequence	0003 SalesOrg/Customer
	After double-clicking this value, you can see that it has exclusive access to sales organization and customer number. The fields used are VKORG (sales organization) and KNDNR (Sold-to party). This access sequence will be suitable for our purposes.
Access to conditions	True
Default values tab	
Dispatch time	Send immediately
Transmission medium	6 EDI
Partner functions	SP Sold-to party
Processing routines for this output	
Program	RSNASTED
Form routine	EDI_PROCESSING

Table 2.9 Output Type BA01—Details

After checking the output type BA01, you know that it is suitable for IDoc creation and can be used in the next sections.

2.5.2 Selecting a Proper Procedure

Sending an order confirmation is maintained by the V10000 procedure. You have to ensure that your output type is present or add it if a new one has been created. You could also attach what is called a *requirement*; that is, a small piece of ABAP code that determines whether the output should be created before checking the condition tables. Proceed as follows:

1. To perform this activity, select the V1 application again, and click the PROCE-DURES button from the main screen of Transaction NACE.

2. Next, select procedure V10000 (ORDER OUTPUT) and select the CONTROL tab at the left (see Figure 2.44). You have to check whether output BA01 is in the list.

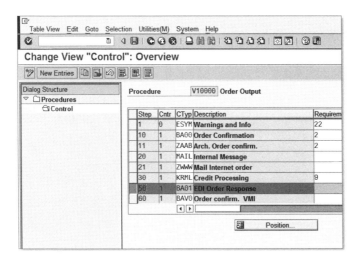

Figure 2.44 Outputs Assigned to Procedure V10000

3. If the output is not listed, go to edit mode and click the NEW ENTRIES button. In the STEP field, enter the next free number. In the CNTR field, enter "1" (this field is not used in output determination but you have to fill it). Then, enter the output type (BA01), and click the SAVE icon.

In this step, you have ensured that output type BA01 is attached to the procedure for sales order confirmation.

2.5.3   Creating Entries in Condition Record Tables

After configuring these technical settings, you have to enter business rules and de-cide to whom the EDI order acknowledgement should be sent. You have to design a condition table for the previously chosen access sequence and fill it with values. Proceed as follows:

1. From the main screen of Transaction NACE, select the appropriate application (V1) and then click the CONDITION RECORDS button.

2. A list of outputs should appear. Select BA01, or another output type if you have created a new output type in the previous step.

3. Output BA01 has an access sequence 003 with one condition table (on the SALES ORGANIZATION and SOLD-TO PARTNER fields). In the selection screen, enter the appropriate SALES ORGANIZATION from which you want to send IDocs (see Figure 2.45).

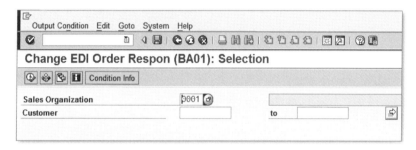

Figure 2.45 Selection Screen of a Condition Record for BA01 Output

4. In the next screen, enter the partner numbers for which IDocs have to be sent. Also enter a partner function (PARTF).

   In our example (see Figure 2.46), we entered CUSTOMER number 10001 and de-cided to send the IDoc for the SP role and partner number 1001 (for partner profile purposes).

By entering this condition record, you ensure that if someone from sales organi-zation 001 modifies the sales order for customer 10001, the information about it will be sent in an IDoc message as a sales order confirmation. But first, you have to set up a partner profile.

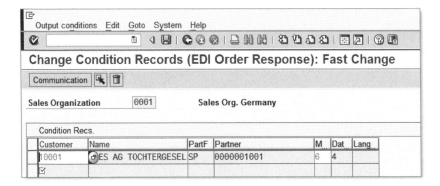

Figure 2.46 Detailed View of a Condition Record

2.5.4 Configuring the Partner Profile

The last setting in our configuration is creating the appropriate partner profile. As with the previous example, you have to add a partner profile for customer 10001 (KU) and then add an outgoing message. Proceed as follows:

1. Start Transaction WE20.

2. Place the cursor on PARTNER TYPE KU, and click the NEW button.

3. Add partner number 100001, and type KU.

4. Add the outgoing configuration for the ORDRSP message. You can find the appropriate settings in Table 2.10.

Field	Value
Message type	ORDRSP
Partner type	KU (Customer)
Partner function	SP (Sold-to party)
Output mode	Transfer IDoc immed.
Basic type	Orders05
Port	Select an appropriate port. This setting depends on your system landscape.

Table 2.10 Partner Profile for Outgoing ORDRSP IDoc

Field	Value
Message Control tab	
Application	V1 (Sales)
Output type	BA01
Process code	SD10

Table 2.10 Partner Profile for Outgoing ORDRSP IDoc (cont.)

2.5.5 Testing the Configuration

After configuring all of these settings, you can test whether IDocs are being created. To do so, create a new sales order for the selected customer and sales organization. In our test case, that is sales organization 0001 and customer 10001. Sales orders are maintained by Transactions VA01 (Create), VA02 (Modify), and VA03 (Display).

1. Enter the ORGANIZATIONAL DATA in the first screen, as shown in Figure 2.47.

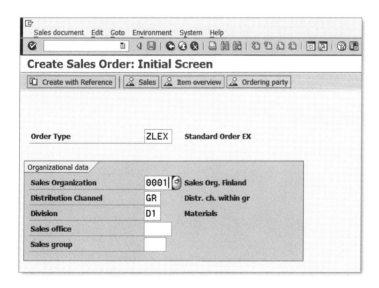

Figure 2.47 Main Screen of Transaction VA01 (Sales Area Data)

2. Next, enter the customer numbers into the SOLD-TO PARTY and SHIP-TO PARTY fields (see Figure 2.48).

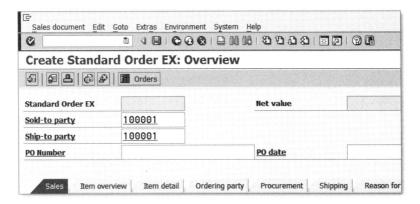

Figure 2.48 Transaction VA01—Entering Partners

3. Finally, from the menu, select EXTRAS • OUTPUT • HEADER • EDIT. If the system, as shown in Figure 2.49, submits the message automatically, it means that everything was configured properly. If not, try to add the output manually and read the warning messages.

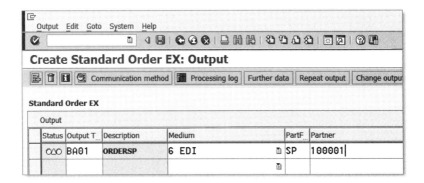

Figure 2.49 EDI Output from a Sales Order

4. Save the order, and look for the IDoc in Transaction WE02. There, you should find a new outgoing IDoc message.

After completing the Customizing in this section, you have succeeded in sending a sales order confirmation via IDoc. The next section will explain how to send the next message: the outbound delivery.

2.6   Outbound Delivery

The goal of this section is to configure outgoing DESADV IDoc messages. The purpose of DESADV is informing partners about delivery creation. Although this message is rarely used, we will show you how to configure the SD component to send this type of message.

After completing the configuration steps, the IDocs will be created in time for the user to save the delivery document. The process will look like the diagram in Figure 2.50.

Figure 2.50 Delivery Flow

As in previous cases, the configuration begins by opening Transaction NACE and selecting application V2 (DELIVERY). The steps are as follows:

1. Selecting or creating output types.

2. Adding the output type to the appropriate procedure.

3. Maintaining the condition record.

4. Defining the partner profile.

5. Testing the configuration.

You will learn about these steps in more detail in the following sections.

2.6.1   Selecting or Creating Output Types

Selecting or creating output types involves certain steps, as follows:

1. You will again start with the output types, where you can create a new one or select an existing one. Take a look at LAVA—OUTG. SHIP. NOTIFICA. by clicking the OUTPUT TYPES button in Transaction NACE. Then double-click the LAVA row. This type is ready for EDI communication.

2. Let us examine the appropriate details (see Table 2.11).

Fields	Value and description
Access sequence	0005 (SalesOrg/Customer) has exclusive access to Sales Organization and Customer Number with no requirements. The used fields are VKORG (Sales organization) and KUNWE (Ship-to party).
Access to conditions	True
Dispatch time	Send immediately *4*
Transmission medium	EDI *6*
Partner functions	SH (Ship-to party) and SP (Sold-to party)
Processing routine for EDI	Program RSNASTED, form routine EDI_PROCESSING

Table 2.11 LAVA Output Type

3. Next, take a look at the requirements. They determine whether the output is created. The requirements are attached to Accesses in the Access Sequence. To view an access sequence, in the output type screen, click the access sequence value twice (see Figure 2.51). The list of possible requirements for output creation of outgoing deliveries is shown in Table 2.12.

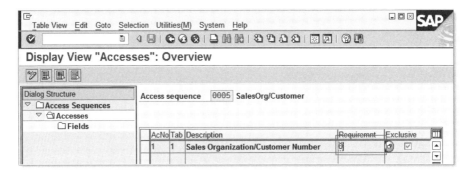

Figure 2.51 Details of Access Sequence 0005

Number and name	Description
1. Delivery GI posted	Check if goods issue has been posted for the delivery.
2. Delivery note	No output, if the credit block is set.

Table 2.12 List of Usable Requirements for Outgoing Delivery

Number and name	Description
10. Credit check block	Sales order blocked due to credit check.
32. WM transfer order	Output should be created if the delivery is relevant for warehouse.
35. Good issue posted/packed	If goods issue has been posted for the delivery and at least some of the items have been packed, then the output should be created.

Table 2.12 List of Usable Requirements for Outgoing Delivery (cont.)

In this section, you have checked that LAVA output will be suitable for the configuration and have seen the possible requirements for changing standard system behavior to generate an output.

2.6.2   Adding the Output Type to the Appropriate Procedure

To have the sample configuration work properly, the chosen output type has to be added to a procedure. For outgoing delivery output, this is the V10000 (header output) procedure, an SAP standard output. You can also add a requirement (see Figure 2.52). For example purposes, we have chosen "3" in the REQUIREMENT field. This will ensure that no output to client will be set in case of a credit block at a customer account.

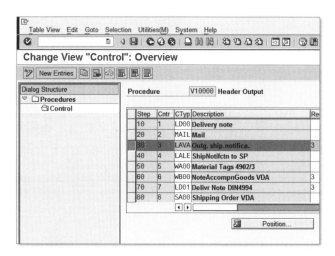

Figure 2.52 Output Types Assigned to V10000

Now that you have chosen the LAVA output and checked whether it is connected with procedure V10000, you have to maintain condition tables and fill them with records.

2.6.3   Maintaining the Condition Records

After selecting the new output type and adding it to the V10000 procedure, you have to maintain the condition record: the group of values for each IDoc that has to be generated. Proceed as follows:

1. Return to the main screen of Transaction NACE and click the OUTPUT TYPES button.

2. Select output type LAVA and click NEXT.

3. You can now enter the appropriate values for keys defined in the condition tables. You will derive these keys from the access sequence connected to the output type. In the beginning of that procedure, at the selection screen, enter the sales organization. In our test case this is 0001, but you can choose what is appropriate for your configuration. Click NEXT (see Figure 2.53).

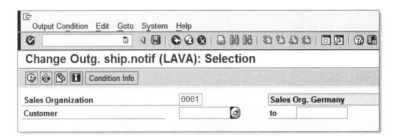

Figure 2.53 Selection Screen for a Condition Record

4. Next, enter the SHIP-TO PARTNER number for which the IDoc has to be generated. You also have to input how the IDoc has to be read by partner profiles. For our example, IDocs will have the partner function SH (ship to partner). We have also inserted 6 EDI for the MEDIUM and 4 CREATING IMMEDIATELY for DATE/TIME (see Figure 2.54).

Figure 2.54 Details of a Condition Record

After this step, the system will look in condition records and decide whether to attach IDoc output for certain deliveries.

2.6.4 Defining the Partner Profile

The next step is the partner profile definition. Proceed as follows:

1. Run Transaction WE20. Create the group for messages for the customer (KU) with the PARTNER NO. 1000 by clicking the NEW icon (see Figure 2.55).

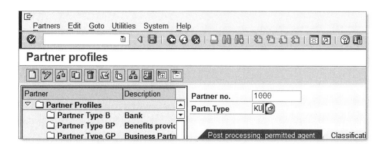

Figure 2.55 Partner Profile for Customer 1000

2. You can then add parameters for an outbound message.

Figure 2.56 shows a screenshot of the partner profile outlined in Table 2.13.

Figure 2.56 DESADV Outgoing Partner Profile

Field	Value
Message type	DESADV
Partner type	KU (customer)
Partner function	SH (vendor)
Output mode	Transfer IDoc immed.
Basic type	DELVRY03
Port	Select a proper port. This depends on your system landscape.
Message Control tab	
Application	V2 (shipping)
Output type	LAVA
Process code	DELV

Table 2.13 Outgoing Partner Profile for DESADV IDoc

2.6.5 Testing the Configuration

To test the IDoc for the creation of the outbound delivery, enter Transaction VL01N. As in other SD transactions, VL02N is for modifying deliveries and VL03N for displaying them. Deliveries are usually created in reference to sales orders. Proceed as follows:

1. First, enter the order number and the delivery date in the selection screen. The delivery date is the same as the delivery date for the items of the sales order.

2. Next, because of your specific system settings, you will probably have to enter additional data such as batches or serial numbers for delivering products. You must comply with the instructions given by the system.

3. After filling out all necessary fields, look at the output control (from the menu, select EXTRAS • DELIVERY OUTPUT • HEADER). There should be a proposal for an EDI message. Take a look at Figure 2.57, where we show the result of this activity.

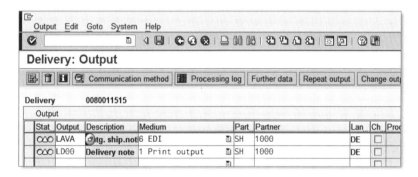

Figure 2.57 Messages Created from a Delivery Document

4. Save your delivery (click the SAVE icon), and go to Transaction WE02 to locate the IDoc that has been created.

This section should bring you closer to configuring IDocs from output deliveries. We will now show you the last document from standard SD flow: SALES ORDER • OUTPUT DELIVERY • INVOICE.

2.7   Outbound Invoice

The last document chosen as an example in this book is a sales invoice. The creation and posting of an invoice will cause the creation of an `INVOIC` IDoc, this time derived from the SD component (see Figure 2.58).

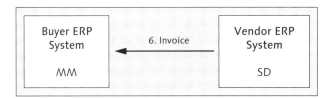

Figure 2.58 Invoicing Process Flow

The configuration procedure is very similar to those of other SD-EDI documents and consists of the following steps:

1. Selecting or creating output types.

2. Adding an output type to the appropriate procedure.

3. Creating a condition table.

4. Creating entries in a partner profile.

5. Testing the configuration.

The following sections will outline these steps in detail.

2.7.1   Selecting or Creating Output Types

The outgoing invoice is represented in Transaction NACE as V3 BILLING. The EDI/IDoc-enabled output type has to have at least one partner with medium 6 EDI, program `RSNASTED` in processing routines, and the `EDI_PROCESSING` form. In case of inadequate access to the access sequence, you can create a new access sequence. To do so, select the standard output access `RD00`. You can find the detailed specification in Table 2.14.

In this step, you have selected the output type, which will be used as the basis for the rest of the configuration.

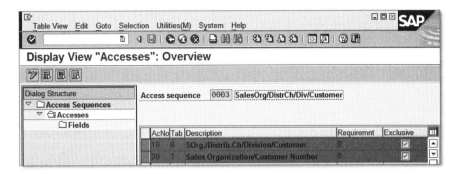

Figure 2.59 Access Sequence 003 Details, Selected for an Invoice

2.7.2 Adding Output Types to the Appropriate Procedure

To add the output type to the appropriate procedure, enter Transaction NACE. Select V3 BILLING, and click the PROCEDURES button. For the EDI invoice, you can use the V10000 BILLING OUTPUT procedure. Select it, and access the CONTROL tab in the tree at the left side of screen.

You have to ensure that RD00 (or any other output type you select) is on the list. You can also add a requirement (see Figure 2.60). One of these is *62*: This entry ensures that the IDoc or any other form of output is only created when the accounting document has been properly posted. It is not a good idea to send an invoice to the partner without being sure that the invoice was posted. If that happens, the invoice has no legal validity.

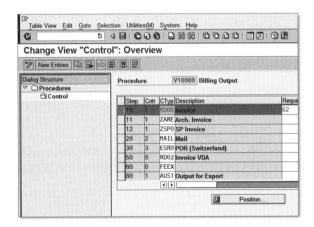

Figure 2.60 Output Types for Procedure V100000 (App V3)

General data tab	
Access sequence	0003 SalesOrg/DistrCh/Div/Customer
	After double-clicking the value 0003, you can see that it has two exclusive accesses with no requirements. The condition tables belonging to this access sequence have the exclusive indicator turned on. Thus, you can configure the system so that in some cases it will generate IDoc invoices and in other cases printouts. (If you are interested in doing this, refer to Section 2.8.)
	You can see the definition of this access sequence in Figure 2.59.
Access to conditions	True
At partner functions section	
Transmission medium	6 EDI
Partner functions	LS (logical system) and SP (sold-to party)
Processing routines for this output	
Program	RSNASTED
Form routine	EDI_PROCESSING

Table 2.14 RD00 Output Type Details

2.7.3 Creating a Condition Table

You now have to enter the access values in an access sequence that will result in the creation of an IDoc. Proceed as follows:

1. From the main screen of Transaction NACE, select V3, and click the CONDITION RECORDS button.

2. Select output RD00 (or the output type you have created) by double-clicking it.

3. The KEY COMBINATION window appears (see Figure 2.61). As you saw previously, the output type has two different access options: one with a sales organization, distribution channel, division and customer; the second without a distribution channel or division. An "exclusive" indicator is activated so that when the condition from the first condition table is present, the second will not be processed. For our example, we are using the model based on the first condition (SORG./DISTRIB.CH/DIVISION/CUSTOMER).

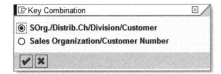

Figure 2.61 Possible Condition Tables for RD00 Output

This configuration model can be used to create two different documents from the same output type. For example, an invoice created in certain distribution channels can be sent via EDI and another can remain in paper form. This is possible because the transmission medium is defined exactly at the condition record level.

In the next screen (see Figure 2.62), enter MEDIUM "6" (EDI) and DATE "4" (immediately).

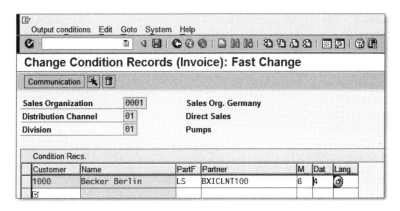

Figure 2.62 Creating a Condition Record

This time, you select the logical system (LS) for the partner function and enter the buyer's system from your landscape. This method is preferable if you have many different condition records for which the receiver is the same technical system (connected with a partner profile through the definition of a port). In this case, you do not have to create as many partner profiles as you do condition records.

After this step, the system will look for the condition records, and if they are fulfilled, the IDoc output will be submitted. Next, you have to connect the output with technical connection details; therefore, you have to maintain a partner profile.

2.7.4 Creating Entries in Partner Profiles

The last step in the EDI outgoing invoice configuration is the creation of a partner profile. The condition record has been prepared for the logical system, and you now have to add an appropriate entry in the partner profile (Transaction WE20).

1. Place the cursor on LS, and click the NEW icon. Next, enter the appropriate logical system name; in our case, it is BXICLNT100. In our test case, we decided to send INVOIC IDocs to our SAP NetWeaver PI server.

2. Now, add a new message to the outbound parameters by clicking the '+' icon and entering the values outlined in Table 2.15.

Field	Value
Message type	INVOIC
Partner type	LS (logical system)
Partner function	LS (logical system)
Output mode	Transfer IDoc immed.
Basic type	INVOIC02
Port	Select an appropriate port. This setting depends on your system landscape.
Message Control tab	
Application	V3 (billing)
Output type	RD00
Process code	SD09

Table 2.15 Partner Profile for Outbound Invoice

3. For the V3 application and the INVOIC message, two useful process codes exist (see Figure 2.63):

   ▸ **SD09**
   This code is used for external communication.

   ▸ **SD08**
   This code is for internal use. Internal use refers to an inter-company process, for example, a process whereby IDocs are exchanged in the same system be-

tween different company codes. Selecting SD08 ensures that outgoing IDocs will not be stored in the database, and you will not see them in Transaction WE02.

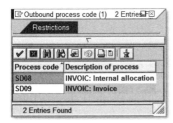

Figure 2.63 Process Codes for an Outgoing Invoice

The partner profile will join the selected message type (RD00) in the IDoc interface.

2.7.5   Testing the Configuration

When testing, you have to create a new invoice with data like that entered in the condition record. In our example, this included SOrg. 0001, Distrib.Ch. 01, Division 01, Customer 1000. In SD, invoices are generally created in reference to a sales order (invoices for services) or an outgoing delivery (invoices for products). Therefore, you have to create the appropriate documents. The following transactions are useful for this purpose:

▶ **VA01**
Used for creating sales orders or other sales documents such as example returns.

▶ **VL01N**
Used for creating outbound deliveries.

▶ **VF01**
Used for creating sales invoices.

After creating an invoice document, you can take a look at the output that was determined. Go to the SAP main menu, and select Goto • Header • Output (or press ⇧+F8). You should see an output proposed that is similar to the one shown in Figure 2.64.

After posting an invoice, the IDoc should be created and you can see it in Transaction WE02. If you cannot see it, try to add the output manually (as shown in Figure 2.64) and read the warnings that are generated.

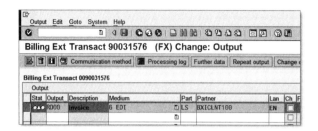

Figure 2.64 Output Messages from an Invoice Document

The INVOIC message was the last real-life example in this section and chapter. As you can see, the procedures for generating inbound and outbound IDocs are similar, and you can also experiment with other business documents.

For the technical details of setting up a configuration for other documents (required applications, procedures, output types, and so on), refer to the section called ALE/EDI Business Processes at *http://help.sap.com*. You can also use the following link: *http://help.sap.com/saphelp_nw04/helpdata/en/dc/6b7cac43d711d18 93e0000e8323c4f/frameset.htm*. Note that it is rather complicated trying to find this section by using a search tool.

2.8   Extension of Condition Tables

All of the examples we have presented in this chapter have made use of existing conditions. But what if your demands for outgoing IDoc configuration are more sophisticated and cannot be defined by existing models? In this case, you have to create our own model consisting of the following:

▶ Condition table (or tables)

▶ Access sequence

▶ Output type

Because you should not modify original SAP entries, creating new condition tables means you also need new access sequences and output types.

Creating new condition tables, access sequences, and output types can be carried out in Transaction SPRO. The paths for all of the types of documents presented in this book are similar, but you will find them in different branches for the SAP SD and SAP MM components (see Figure 2.65 and Figure 2.66).

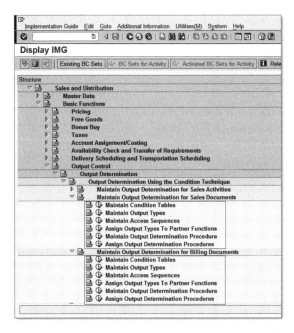

Figure 2.65 Path for Maintaining Output Determination for Sales Documents

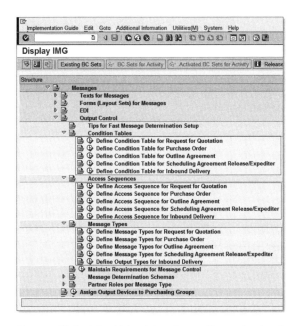

Figure 2.66 Path for Maintaining Output Determination for Material Documents

2.8.1   Creating a Condition Table

We will start with creating a new condition table for a sales document. Proceed as follows:

1. In the appropriate tree, select MAINTAIN OUTPUT DETERMINATION FOR SALES DOCUMENTS • MAINTAIN CONDITION TABLES.

2. Click FIELD CATALOG: MESSAGES FOR SALES DOCUMENTS (see Figure 2.67).

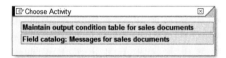

Figure 2.67 Condition Table Menu for Sales Document

3. In the next screen, look for keys that could be used to create condition records. In some cases, depending on the business needs, the list might be insufficient, and you would have to extend it by clicking the NEW ENTRIES button.

4. Then, press F4 on FIELD to open the list (see Figure 2.68).

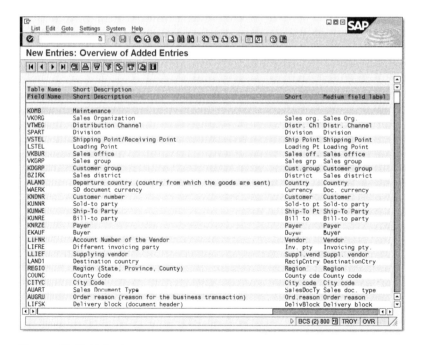

Figure 2.68 Field Catalog

The list of fields is impressive, but some of the fields need to be programmed by special ABAP user exits. This is why they are not present in the condition-record structures that are filled during the creation of business documents in transactions and compared with condition records.

5. The procedure of selecting new fields requires you to add an append structure with the new field to the condition record structure and implement a special user exit. If the field name is identical to the field in the original table (e.g., Table VBAK with a sales order header), the user exit is not necessary because original programs copy values via the MOVE-CORRESPONDING command. This ABAP command copies—between two structures—all fields with the same names. The list of communication structures that have to be extended by new fields is shown in Table 2.16. This structure should not be directly extended but used only with the append structures.

6. The routines and user exits for assigning new fields are found in the programs RVCOMFZZ, RVCOMFZ1, and RVCOMFZ4; you can study these programs by running Transaction SE38. In their source code, you can easily learn for which fields the structure is responsible.

7. After extending the field catalog, you can create a new condition table. Select MAINTAIN OUTPUT CONDITION TABLE FOR SALES DOCUMENTS from the previous pop-up window, and on the next screen, select CREATE from the menu.

Structure	Include	Description
KOMKBK1	KOMKBZ1	Output Determination Communication Area CAS Appl. K1
KOMKBV1	KOMKBZ3	Output Determination Communication Area Header Appl. V1
KOMKBV2	KOMKBZ4	Output Determination Communication Area Header Appl. V2
KOMKBV3	KOMKBZ5	Output Determination Communication Area Header Appl. V3
KOMKBV5	KOMKBZF	Communication Structure for Output Control Groups Appl. V5

Table 2.16 List of Condition Record Communication Structures and Appends

8. For the input in the upper area of the screen, enter a number for the new table (from 501 to 999), and for the input in the lower area of the screen, use F4 help. Select the table most similar to the new one (see Figure 2.69).

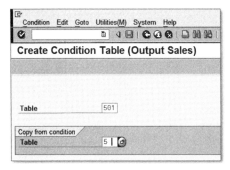

Figure 2.69 Creating a Condition Table (Step 1)

9. In the next screen, double-clicking the field at the right side will add a new key field to the table that was created (see Figure 2.70).

Figure 2.70 Creating a Condition Table (Step 2)

10. After saving, you should see the screen shown in Figure 2.71. It means that the system created new condition tables and generated programs through which the tables can be filled with data (condition records). This program is used in Transaction NACE.

Status	Note
Information	805 Table B510 has been saved
Information	748 Reports and screens for table B 510 marked for generation

Figure 2.71 Status of Creating New Condition Tables

In this step, you have created a new condition table. But you cannot use it yet in output type determination because it is not attached to any access sequence. In the next section, we will show you how to perform this attachment.

2.8.2 Access Sequence

The access sequence is—as you know already—the connection between a condition table and an output type. Moreover, as you know, it is possible to assign multiple condition tables to one access sequence. This could mean, for example, linking different forms of output (printout, fax, or EDI) or printout with different languages to a single output type. The second function of an access sequence is to bind fields from communication structures to keys from condition tables. This is mandatory for our new condition table. Proceed as follows:

1. Select MAINTAIN ACCESS SEQUENCE (look at Figure 2.65 for the entire path) for sales documents (from Transaction SPRO), and click the NEW ENTRIES button.

2. Now, add a unique identifier from the Z-namespace and a description. It is common to enter all fields that appear in chosen accesses in the name of the access sequence (see the example in Figure 2.72).

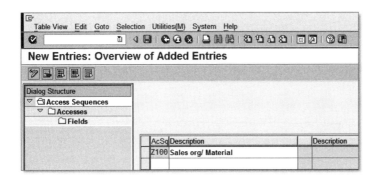

Figure 2.72 Creating an Access Sequence

3. After saving, you can get ready for the next step: adding accesses to the sequence. Select the newly added access sequence, and click the ACCESSES root in the tree. Next, click the NEW ENTRIES button again.

4. Now, enter the order and the condition table number (see Figure 2.73). You also can attach a requirement (if you want to add ABAP code to control system behavior).

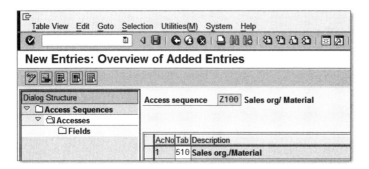

Figure 2.73 Adding a Condition Table to an Access Sequence

5. Checking the EXCLUSIVE option ensures that if the condition is fulfilled during runtime, the next condition is not checked. If you have only one condition table, this becomes irrelevant. In the example presented, we have left this option unchecked.

6. Click SAVE, and bind the key fields from the condition table to the communication structure. In this case, select the added table and click FIELDS in the tree (see Figure 2.74).

7. The system automatically binds VKORG to KOMKBV1-BKORG and MATNR to the corresponding field, but you can check the assignment by selecting a field and clicking the FIELD CATALOG button (see Figure 2.75).

8. You can also simplify the condition by entering a constant value, as shown in Figure 2.76.

9. By activating the INIT checkbox, you ensure that the system does not access the condition if the field in the document header/item is blank or zero (see Figure 2.77).

After completing the access sequence, you can attach it to an output type and use it in an output determination (by filling in condition records).

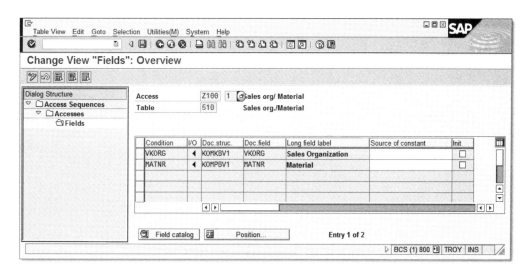

Figure 2.74 Assigning Communication Fields to Control-Table Keys

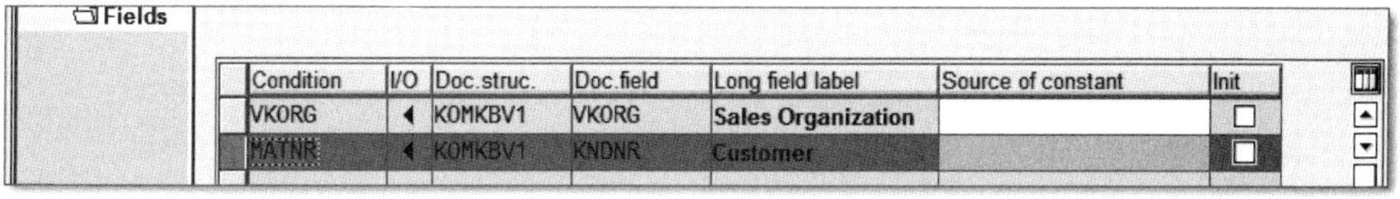

	Condition	I/O	Doc.struc.	Doc.field	Long field label	Source of constant	Init	
Fields	VKORG	◄	KOMKBV1	VKORG	Sales Organization		☐	
	MATNR	◄	KOMKBV1	KNDNR	Customer		☐	

Figure 2.75 Field Mapping

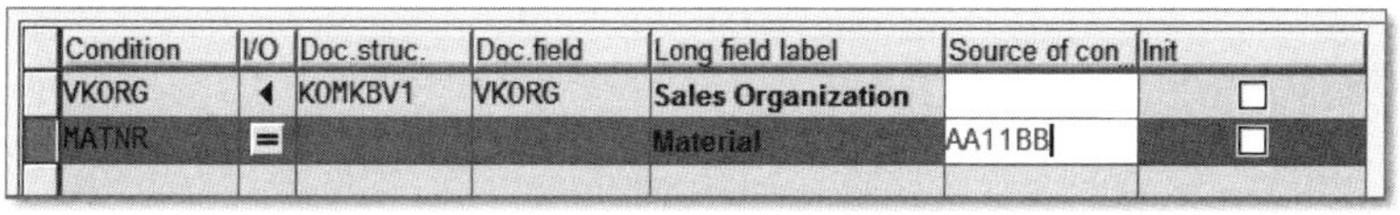

Condition	I/O	Doc.struc.	Doc.field	Long field label	Source of con	Init
VKORG	◄	KOMKBV1	VKORG	Sales Organization		☐
MATNR	=			Material	AA11BB	☐

Figure 2.76 Mapping a Constant Value to a Field

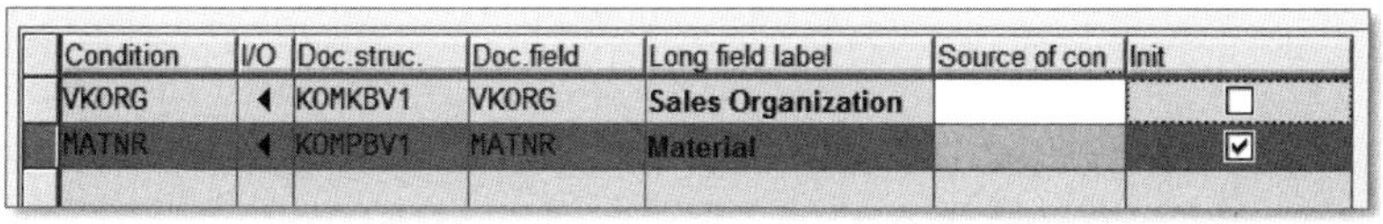

Condition	I/O	Doc.struc.	Doc.field	Long field label	Source of con	Init
VKORG	◄	KOMKBV1	VKORG	Sales Organization		☐
MATNR	◄	KOMPBV1	MATNR	Material		☑

Figure 2.77 Setting the Init Flag

2.8.3 Output Type

The last step is creating a new output type. The easiest way is to make a copy from another EDI-enabled output type. Then, enter the new access sequence. From here on, you can use your own model while designing condition records.

You now know how to create more sophisticated rules for output determination. As a result, you can use document fields not provided by SAP in standard condition tables.

2.9 Summary

In this chapter, we have shown you how to send and receive IDocs with transactional data from an SAP ERP system. You learned how to configure interfaces on the SAP ECC side with the most popular logistic scenarios from the SAP SD and SAP MM components. In Chapter 3, we will explain how to send and receive IDocs with master data.

3   Master Data Distribution

In Chapter 2, you learned how to configure an SAP ECC system to send and receive transactional data. However, if there is a need to exchange transactional data there is also very often a requirement of exchanging master data.

As you have seen in previous chapters, you can use MC to send transactional data. However, this tool cannot be used for exchanging master data; instead, there are two procedures in SAP ECC for distributing master data, as follows:

▶ Sending master data directly.

▶ Distributing master data with the Shared Master Data (SMD) tool.

Both require an ALE layer and a distribution model to produce IDocs. First, we will focus on the differences and purposes of these two procedures. The configuration of the distribution model in the ALE layer will be explained later in this chapter.

Sending Master Data Directly

A set of standard reports is used to distribute different master data objects to other systems. These reports can be run manually or they can be scheduled and run automatically in the background. These reports often provide selection criteria and it is possible to customize which object should be distributed (e.g., lowering the amount of data by number ranges, plant, etc.).

These reports are used mostly for initial load purposes (when the interface is at go-live and other systems should be provided with the entire set of data) but can also be used as a background job to periodically supply the external system with up to date data. The limitation of this method is the amount of data. For example, it is not effective to use this tool every day to exchange hundreds of thousands of records when the actual changes concern only a few of the records. For this purpose it is more suitable to use the SMD tool, which will be described in the next section. You will find a list of different master data objects and the corresponding transactions in which to send them in Table 3.1.

Shared Master Data Tool

Using the SMD tool is a more sophisticated method to build master data interfaces. It allows for "delta" exchange. This means that the system sends only new records and changes to existing master data objects, not the entire data. This method is the common method for building highly efficient, message-driven interfaces for master data.

To learn how this method works, we have to look at the *SAP change document interface*. In SAP ECC, when a master data object is created or modified, a *change document* is created. Change documents consist of a header and different positions. The *header* consists of the document number, the type of change (creation or modification), and the date and the change number. *Positions* consist of fields that were modified with their old and new values. Technically, change documents are stored in CDHDR and CDPOS tables. There is also a set of standard function modules that are invoked in SAP transactions to fill these tables.

The change document interface is a part of SAP ECC and is used for different purposes. One of the recipients is shared master data, using *change pointers*. The change pointers mechanism consists of a set of customizing steps in which you can specify that changes in master data objects of a particular type should be distributed by IDocs. The procedure is as follows:

1. A user creates or changes a master data object.

2. A change document interface is started and a change document is recorded into the database.

3. The change document is transferred to the SMD tool. If a change pointer to a particular master object is switched on, the change pointer is recorded into the database

Technically, change pointers are stored in BDCP and BDCPS tables (with Web Application Server 6.10 and higher it could also be a BDCP2 table). To create IDocs in the event of changes in master data, you need to periodically invoke the RBDMIDOC report. This report reads the change pointers table and produces master IDocs. The status of processed change pointers changes to *read* (to avoid sending the same changes more than once).

The master IDoc is handed over by the ALE layer, which creates regular IDocs and—because of the distribution model (see the next sections)—sends them to the appropriate receivers. The entire process is illustrated in Figure 3.1.

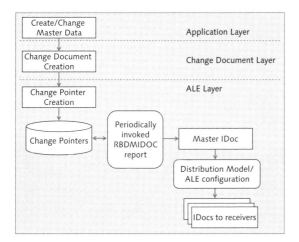

Figure 3.1 Generating IDocs of Master Data Changes

These two procedures (sending master data directly and using the SMD tool) are often combined. Reports for sending master data directly are used for initial load (at go-live) and change pointers are used to distribute changes during normal system usage.

You will see in the next sections how to configure these elements. In our example, we will cover the configuration for sending customers, vendors and material master data. We will exchange data between two SAP ERP systems, but the second system could also be an external, non-SAP system connected with SAP ERP via SAP NetWeaver PI. In a real business scenario, the SAP ERP system is often a master system for master data management. In this scenario, all changes to this data take place in the SAP ERP system and are propagated by SAP NetWeaver PI to other systems in landscape. Therefore, in this chapter, we will focus on sending master data from SAP ERP. However, at the end of the chapter, you will find information on how to receive master data using a distribution model to a second SAP ERP system.

3.1   Change Pointers

As you already know, change pointers are used to inform SMD that some objects have changed and that it is time to produce an IDoc. Change pointers are configured as follows:

1. First, you have to activate change pointers in general. To accomplish this, you have to open Transaction SALE (most of the configuration in this chapter will be performed in Transaction SALE), which can be seen in Figure 3.2.

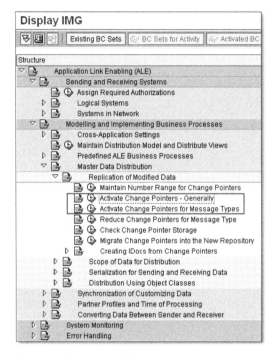

Figure 3.2 Transaction SALE

2. Next, select APPLICATION LINKING ENABLING (ALE) • MODELLING AND IMPLE-MENTING BUSINESS PROCESSES • MASTER DATA DISTRIBUTION • REPLICATION OF MODIFIED DATA • ACTIVATING CHANGE POINTERS • GENERALLY.

3. Then, select the checkbox CHANGE POINTERS ACTIVATED – GENERALLY and save your selection (see Figure 3.3).

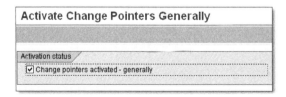

Figure 3.3 Activating Change Pointers In General

4. After having activated change pointers in general, you need to turn on change pointers for particular objects. As mentioned, we have chosen customers, vendors and material data. From the same position in the tree in Transaction SALE, select ACTIVATE CHANGE POINTERS FOR MESSAGE TYPES. This is where you define which master data object changes generate IDocs.

5. From the list, select the IDoc message types CREMAS (for vendors), DEBMAS (for customers) and MATMAS (for material master), select the checkboxes in the ACTIVATE column, and save your changes. As shown in Figure 3.4, within the list, you can see the different IDoc message types you can activate to send IDocs with changes. Table 3.1 contains master data objects and the corresponding IDoc message types.

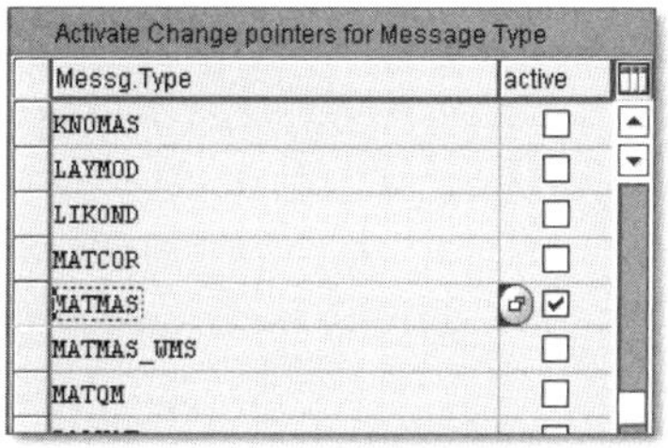

Figure 3.4 Activating Change Pointers for Particular Objects

Master data object	IDoc message type	Transaction to send
Material master	MATMAS	BD10
Vendor	CREMAS	BD14
Customer	DEBMAS	BD12
Product catalog	PRDCAT	–
Price list	PRICAT	–
Price conditions	COND_A	–
Bill of materials (BOM)	BOMMAT	BD30
G/L account	GLMAST	BD18
Cost center	COSMAS	BD16
Cost element	COELEM	BD24

Table 3.1 Different Master Data Objects and the Corresponding IDoc Message Types

The system is now configured to generate change pointers for customers, vendors, and materials. You can verify this making a modification in any material master record (using Transaction MM02) and then opening Transaction SE16 and looking at the last entry in table BDCP (or, depending on the system version, table BDCP2). There should be a record related to your change. Table CDPOS (linked via the field CHANGENR) should show the technical name of the fields you changed, with the old and new values.

The next step is configuring the distribution model. It tells you who will be a receiver of the created IDocs.

3.2 Distribution Model

When change pointers are configured, the system knows that it has to register changes in master data because they will be sent as IDocs. But it does not know who will be the IDoc receiver. The main purpose of the distribution model is to specify receivers for IDocs. It also consists of tools that simplify the entire configuration for sending and receiving master data.

As you know, IDocs can be exchanged directly between SAP systems and non-SAP systems using an integration server such as SAP NetWeaver PI (IDocs are translated into internet standards such as Web Services).

For the direct exchange between two SAP ECC systems, the distribution model allows you to do configure both systems in one place. In this scenario, one system is the sender of a set of master data and the other is the recipient.

For our example, we will assume that we have two SAP ECC systems. One is called BCS and the other is called BE6. The logical names of these systems are BCSCLNT800 and BE6CLNT100. We want to establish interfaces for master data such as material master, vendors, and customers (for which we turned on change pointers in the previous section). The BCSCLNT800 system will be the sender and the BE6CLNT100 system will be the receiver (see Figure 3.5).

When we operate with system names in the distribution model, we use logical systems (refer to Chapter 1 for details). As you remember, logical systems are also managed in Transaction SALE. For this example, you could define a system different from BE6CLNT100 in your landscape. In this case, you need to define the receiver system in the logical systems via Transaction SALE and the path APPLICA-

TION LINK ENABLING (ALE) • SENDING AND RECEIVING SYSTEMS • LOGICAL SYSTEMS •
DEFINE LOGICAL SYSTEM.

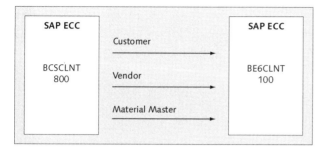

Figure 3.5 Message Flow for the Master Data Scenario

In addition, the sender system (BCSCLNT800) has to be assigned to the client via
SALE • APPLICATION LINK ENABLING (ALE) • SENDING AND RECEIVING SYSTEMS • LOG-
ICAL SYSTEMS • ASSIGN CLIENT TO LOGICAL SYSTEM. (This task is always performed
during the Basis system installation; therefore, you probably do not have to do it
now).

We will now start with the configuration of the distribution model:

1. Log in to BCSCLNT800 (the sender system).

2. Open Transaction SALE and select APPLICATION LINK ENABLING (ALE) • MODEL-
   LING AND IMPLEMENTING BUSINESS PROCESSES • MAINTAIN DISTRIBUTION MODEL
   AND DISTRIBUTE VIEWS (see Figure 3.6).

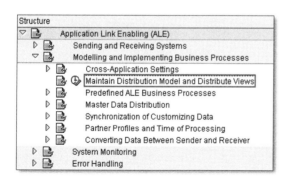

Figure 3.6 Transaction SALE and the Distribution Model

3. Switch to edit mode and click the CREATE MODEL VIEW button.

4. Next, enter a short name, a technical name, and a start and end date for this model (see Figure 3.7). The start and end dates are very useful. If there are known changes that will be made to your system landscape, you can set the end date of the existing model to the date of the landscape changes and prepare a new model with a start date from that point.

Figure 3.7 Creating a New Model

5. Highlight the model, click the ADD MESSAGE TYPE button, and specify SENDER SYSTEM, RECEIVER SYSTEM and MESSAGE TYPE. In our example, the settings would be as follows:

   ▶ Model view: MMVENCUS

   ▶ Sender: BCSCLNT800

   ▶ Receiver: BE6CLNT100

   ▶ Message type: MATMAS (for material master exchange)

6. We also want to send vendors and customers; therefore, repeat this step for these message types as follows:

   ▶ CREMAS (for Vendors)

   ▶ DEBMAS (for Customers)

(Provide the same sender and receiver system as specified previously.) Your screen should look similar to the one shown in Figure 3.8.

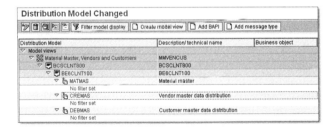

Figure 3.8 Example of a Distribution Model for Material Master, Vendors, and Customers

With the current configuration, all customers, vendors, and materials will be sent. However, it is possible to place filters and thus limit the data that is sent. In our example, we want to send only master data that fulfills filter requirements; therefore, we will place a filter for material master. As you know, different material types can be maintained in SAP ECC. For example, there are finished products (type FERT) and finished goods (type HAVA). We will use material type as a parameter to filter materials, limiting the interface to send only master data of finished products. Proceed as follows:

1. Select the No FILTER SET field under MATMAS and double-click.

2. A new window opens and you can create filters by choosing CREATE FILTER GROUP. After expanding the subtree, you should see all of the possible fields you can use for filtering. For our example, select MATERIAL TYPE and double-click. Next, by using the "+" icon, enter a FERT value. FERT is a standard material type for finished goods.

3. Return to the main screen of the distribution model. You will see that instead of No FILTER SET, DATA FILTER ACTIVE is displayed under MATMAS. Save your changes.

The distribution model is now ready. The following summarizes what we have achieved in this section:

▶ We have created the distribution model and the system BCSCLNT800 will send master data to BE6CLNT100.

▶ The set of data contains material master, vendors, and customers.

▶ By using a filter on material master, we limited the scope of materials to only finished products (FERT material type).

In the next section, we will finish the configuration for the sending system. The missing steps are creating the partner profiles and scheduling a report for IDoc generation.

3.3   Partner Profile for the Distribution Model

As you know from previous chapters, sending IDocs requires an appropriate partner profile. A partner profile is a set of rules that specifies how an IDoc to be sent to a specific receiver should be created (e.g., which program has to be used to create the IDoc, should it be send one by one or in packets, etc.). Refer to Chapter 1 for more general information on this topic.

The advantage of creating a partner profile from the distribution model is that it is possible to generate the profile automatically.

There is a single prerequisite to automatically create partner profiles from the distribution model. You need to have the same name for the sender logical system and an R/3 connection managed in Transaction SM59. This requirement is easy to fulfill because the common naming convention for the R/3 connection is similar to logical system names (refer to Chapter 1 for more information on this topic). To create a partner profile from the distribution model, proceed as follows:

1. Open Transaction SALE and go to MAINTAINING DISTRIBUTION MODEL (APPLICA-TION LINK ENABLING (ALE) • MODELLING AND IMPLEMENTING BUSINESS PROCESSES • MAINTAIN DISTRIBUTION MODEL AND DISTRIBUTE VIEWS). Alternatively, you can open Transaction BD64 directly.

2. In the main screen, select your distribution model (in our example, it is MMVEN-CUS) and choose ENVIRONMENT • GENERATE PARTNER PROFILES from the menu.

3. In the next screen, you can set parameters (see Figure 3.9). The predefined values are fine for our example. Click EXECUTE to begin the creation of partner profiles. The results should be the same as shown in Figure 3.10. The results are:

   ▷ A partner profile has been created for the logical system.

   ▷ The system found that the same R/3 connection name as the logical system name exists (Transaction SM59; refer to Chapter 1 for more information on this transaction) and the port was created. As you learned previously, the connection requires the same name as the logical system to be able to create the partner profile from scratch using this tool.

   ▷ The following outbound messages were added:
     - CREMAS04 for sending vendors
     - DEBMAS06 for sending customers
     - MATMAS05 for sending materials
     - SYNCHON for technical purposes

After generating the partner profile, the scenario for sending master data is almost complete. From here, it is possible to test the scenario for SENDING MASTER DATA DIRECTLY. If you want to send changes in master data automatically, there is one additional step, described in Section 3.4.

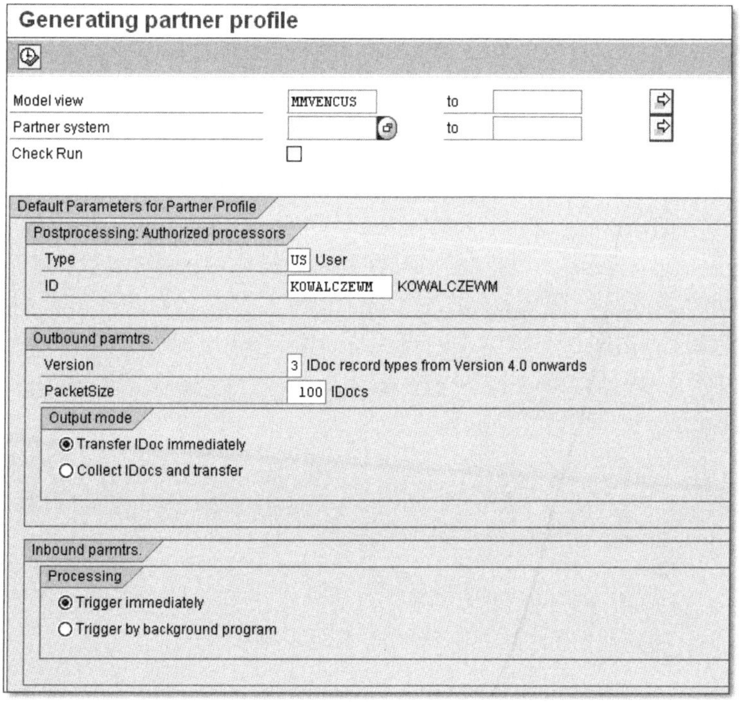

Generating partner profile

⊕

Model view	MMVENCUS	to	⇨
Partner system	⬚	to	⇨
Check Run	☐		

Default Parameters for Partner Profile

Postprocessing: Authorized processors

Type	US	User
ID	KOWALCZEWM	KOWALCZEWM

Outbound parmtrs.

Version	3	IDoc record types from Version 4.0 onwards
PacketSize	100	IDocs

Output mode

◉ Transfer IDoc immediately
○ Collect IDocs and transfer

Inbound parmtrs.

Processing

◉ Trigger immediately
○ Trigger by background program

Figure 3.9 Generating a Partner Profile Directly from the Distribution Model

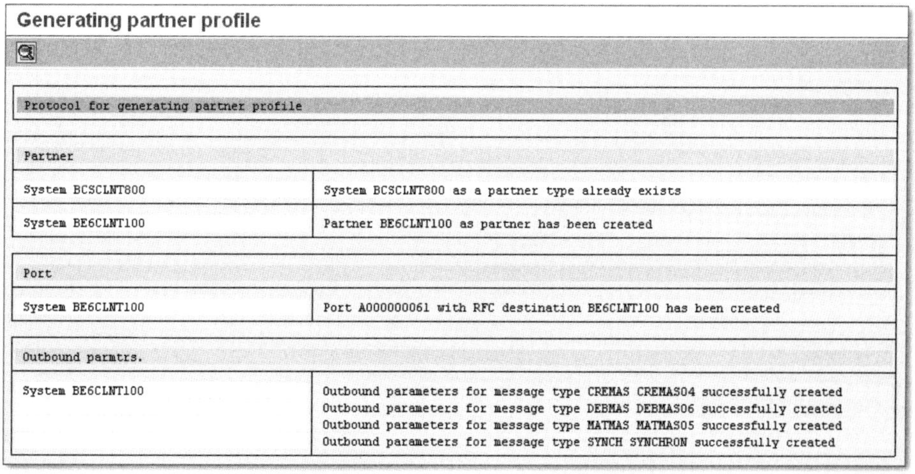

Generating partner profile

🔍

Protocol for generating partner profile

Partner

System BCSCLNT800	System BCSCLNT800 as a partner type already exists
System BE6CLNT100	Partner BE6CLNT100 as partner has been created

Port

System BE6CLNT100	Port A000000061 with RFC destination BE6CLNT100 has been created

Outbound parmtrs.

System BE6CLNT100	Outbound parameters for message type CREMAS CREMAS04 successfully created Outbound parameters for message type DEBMAS DEBMAS06 successfully created Outbound parameters for message type MATMAS MATMAS05 successfully created Outbound parameters for message type SYNCH SYNCHRON successfully created

Figure 3.10 Creating Partner Profiles

To test the scenario SENDING MASTER DATA DIRECTLY, use Transactions BD10, BD12, and BD14 and send one material, vendor, and customer.

3.4 Scheduling Reports

To fully make use of change pointers, you have to schedule the report RBDMIDOC. This report periodically sends any changes collected. Proceed as follows:

1. In Transaction SALE, select APPLICATION LINK ENABLING (ALE) • MODELLING AND IMPLEMENTING BUSINESS PROCESSES • MASTER IDOC DISTRIBUTION • REPLICATION OF MODIFIED DATA • CREATING IDOCS FROM CHANGE POINTERS. In the tree you see two options:

   ▶ CHOOSE/DEFINE VARIANTS

   ▶ SCHEDULE REPORT

2. The first step involves creating a variant for every message of the distribution model for which changes should be sent automatically. Select DEFINE VARIANTS and in the next screen, select GOTO • VARIANTS from the menu.

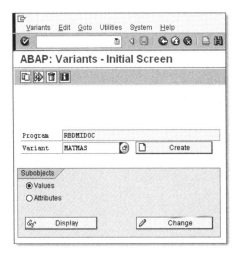

Figure 3.11 Variant Maintenance

3. Next, enter the name of the variant. It is good practice to choose a name similar to the message type for which the variant is being created. Click CREATE (see Figure 3.11).

4. You also have to create variants for the message types MATMAS, DEBMAS and CREMAS.

5. Enter "MATMAS" and click CREATE.

6. In the next screen, enter the MESSAGE TYPE "MATMAS" and click the BACK icon.

7. Click YES in the pop-up to confirm.

8. In the next screen, enter a description for the variant (for example: "Sending MATMAS IDocs") in the field MEANING and click the SAVE button. Repeat this procedure for the message types DEBMAS and CREMAS.

After variant preparation, the second step involves scheduling the report RBDM-IDOC for each message type. Proceed as follows:

1. Go back to Transaction SALE and select SCHEDULE REPORT.

2. In the first screen, enter the job name, for example "Sending MATMAS IDocs" and click START CONDITION.

3. In the next screen, click IMMEDIATE (see Figure 3.12) and click the PERIOD VALUES button.

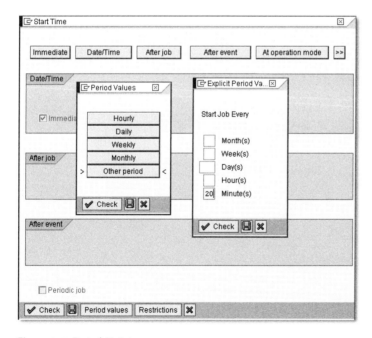

Figure 3.12 Period Maintenance

107

4. You can now specify how often the job will be executed and the time when IDocs with changes will be populated. Click OTHER PERIOD and then enter the time. For our example, specify 20 minutes between two jobs.

5. Click SAVE and go back to the first job creation screen.

6. Next, click the STEP button on the first job creation screen. This is where you will specify the action in the system. In the NAME field you should see the name of the report RBDMIDOC.

7. Select a variant for the report from the previously created variants and save your changes. In our example, we will first use the MATMAS variant (see Figure 3.13).

8. This completes the procedure of scheduling the job. Repeat this procedure for the other messages, DEBMAS and CREMAS. For these, you can specify a different start time so that each starts after the previous job has finished.

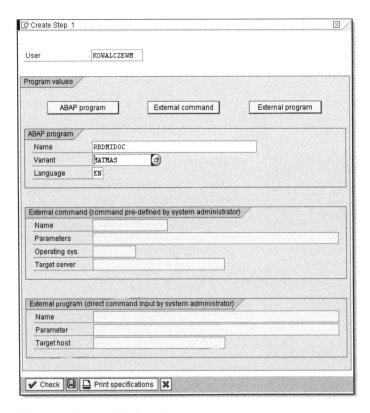

Figure 3.13 The Step Configuration

It is good practice to also schedule report RBDCPCLR for deleting used change pointers. This practice will keep the change pointer tables at a reasonable size. The maintenance of the report is very simple; therefore, this is not explained further in this book.

3.5   Configuring the Production System

Unfortunately, not all of the configuration we have described is automatically added to transport requests. Some of the work has to be done manually in the production system the same way it was done in the development system. We will describe step by step which elements require additional effort.

The activation of the general indicator and of particular change pointers is automatically added to a transport request. However, with the distribution model, it is not as easy. As you know, the model is prepared for particular logical systems. Therefore, in the development system, you should build three different models for the entire landscape (development, quality assurance, and production system). It is good practice to build the model for the development system and perform all tests. If the model fulfills all business requirements, create another one for the quality assurance landscape, using a copy of the development landscape (change only logical system names). If all tests here also complete without issue, use the quality assurance landscape as a reference for the production environment (creating a copy of the quality assurance landscape and changing only logical system names).

To build a model from an existing model, open the MAINTENANCE OF DISTRIBUTION MODEL (using a link from Transaction SALE or using Transaction BD64 directly), go to edit mode, and highlight a model to copy. Then, select EDIT • MODEL VIEW • COPY from the menu.

In the next screen (see Figure 3.14), enter a name and the sending and receiving systems for the next landscape and confirm.

After creating a distribution model copy, you can add the model to the transport request by selecting EDIT • MODEL VIEW • TRANSPORT from the menu.

At each system in the landscape you also need to manually perform the following: Create partner profiles (Section 3.3) and schedule jobs (Section 3.4). Variants for reports are transportable; therefore, you can schedule reports using the same variants as those you created in the development system.

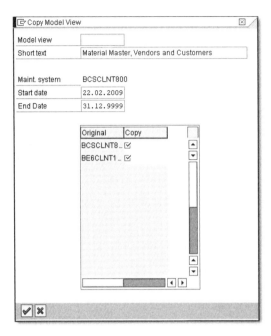

Figure 3.14 Copying an Existing Distribution Model

3.6 The Receiving System

There is another big advantage of using the distribution model versus manual configuration. This book is concerned with SAP NetWeaver PI; however, when the receiving system is another SAP ECC system (without an integration server), it is possible to send the distribution model to the receiving system and import and create all of the necessary configuration for incoming IDocs on the receiving system side.

To send the distribution model, open Transaction BD64 or locate the distribution model in Transaction SALE. Then, select EDIT • MODEL VIEW • DISTRIBUTE from the menu. Select the name of the model you want to distribute. In our example it is MMVENCUS. On the next screen, the system displays a list of the existing logical systems and the receiving system should be highlighted. Confirm in the pop-up screen, and the model should be sent to the second SAP ECC system.

Next, log on to the receiving system and open the distribution model there (using Transaction SALE or directly by using Transaction BD64). The imported model should be visible. In this system, the model has the status *read only* because the master version is located on the other system. However, we do not want to perform any changes in interface logic—our purpose is to generate partner profiles for inbound IDocs. To accomplish this, perform the same steps as those outlined in Section 3.3. From the menu, select ENVIRONMENT • GENERATE PARTNER PROFILES and confirm the generation of the partner profiles in the next screen (see Figure 3.9). As you can see, this function creates the necessary partner profiles from the distribution model for both outgoing and incoming IDocs.

3.7   Summary

This chapter provided you with information on how to create an interface for master data. You were provided with two approaches:

▸ Sending master data directly using predefined reports.

▸ Sending "delta" changes using change pointers.

These two methods require the definition of a distribution model and the creation of partner profiles. Sending "delta" changes also requires special *report scheduling*.

This as well as the previous chapter explained different ways of interfacing transactional documents. As such, they described the most common cases of configuring SAP ECC interfaces.

4 IDoc Monitoring

IDoc monitoring is a very important daily task. The operator has to check the status of incoming and outgoing IDocs and fix any errors. In this chapter, we will present the most common transactions and techniques for monitoring IDoc interfaces in the SAP application system and also how to do the same using SAP Solution Manager if many SAP application systems need to be monitored. In Chapter 5, you will also find out how to monitor IDoc messages from SAP NetWeaver Process Integration (SAP NetWeaver PI).

4.1 Searching for IDocs

To check an IDoc's status and view its data, you can use Transaction WE02. We will run that transaction and see how it looks.

The selection screen makes it possible to filter IDocs by the most important parameters, including:

- Creation date
- Direction (inbound or outbound)
- IDoc number
- Current status
- Basic type
- Logical message
- Message code
- Message function
- Partner port
- Partner number
- Partner type

Figure 4.1 displays the selection screen.

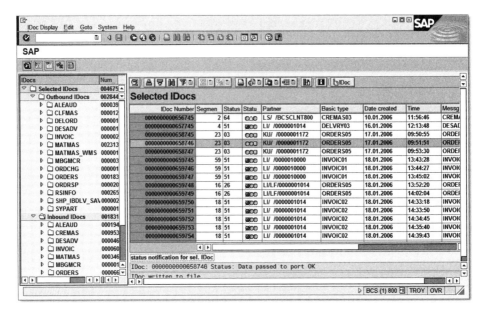

Figure 4.1 Transaction WE02—IDocs List

On the IDoc view screen, (see Figure 4.2) you can find all information concerning IDoc data (IDoc segments) and its processing status in the STATUS RECORDS tree. Double-clicking on the status details opens the status description (see Figure 4.3).

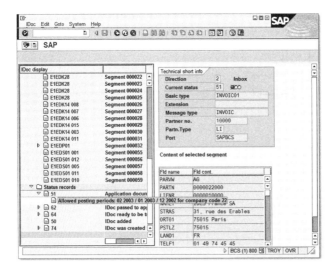

Figure 4.2 Transaction WE02—IDoc Detailed View

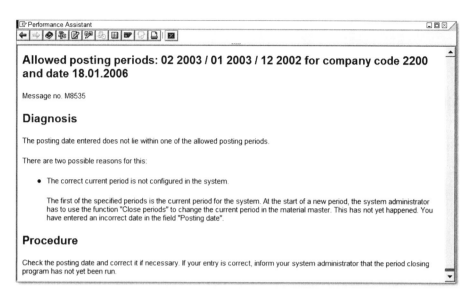

Figure 4.3 Example of a Status View

The detailed status description is very helpful during IDoc debugging. The system sometimes proposes links to the Customizing settings maintenance—activities from Transaction SPRO—that were not correctly prepared.

If you see an error such as MESSAGES FROM IDOC PROCESSING CAN BE FOUND IN AP-PLICATION LOG (see Figure 4.4), you have to double-click on the status number and click the APPLICATION LOG button. This will open a window to display the error messages (see Figure 4.5).

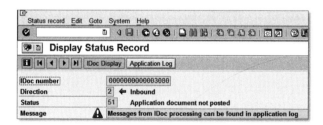

Figure 4.4 IDoc Status with Comment in the Application Log

Transaction WE02 is the basic tool for IDoc monitoring. You should open this transaction a few times each day and check whether all statuses are correct. The next section will explain ways to fix errors if they occur.

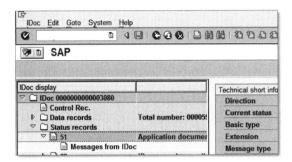

Figure 4.5 Displaying the Application Log

4.2 IDoc Reprocessing $\mathcal{BD87}$

There are cases in which IDoc processing is stopped due to an error in both directions—inbound and outbound. This can have many causes but sometimes simply restarting the IDoc can make it work again. This section will show you how reprocessing can be performed using standard transactions.

4.2.1 Inbound Documents

Some errors in inbound IDoc messages can be repaired by changing the configuration or changing master data, for example, when an order cannot be created because of a non-existing customer. In this case, you have to add a new customer and then reprocess the IDoc message.

After making changes and determining a potential source of a problem, it is possible to reprocess IDocs using Transaction BD87. Let us take a look at the details of this process.

1. Open Transaction BD87 and select the proper time interval, for example, one day.

2. After execution, the screen presents statistics (see Figure 4.6) showing how many IDocs have been processed successfully and how many have errors. The statistic is presented in a tree view.

3. IDocs are reprocessed by selecting a group of IDocs (represented as a row in a tree) and then clicking the PROCESS button. You can only reprocess IDocs that have a red or yellow status. While reprocessing, new statutes are added, as shown in Figure 4.7. This figure shows that some IDocs were posted correctly

Handwritten notes:
MATMAS BD10
CREMAS (V) BD14
DEBMAS (C) BD12
BOWMAT BD30

SAP PM & ABAP Code Niraj Visnoi

SAP ALE and IDOC Transactions

SAP ALE and IDOC Transactions

Home

What is SAP ?

SAP LSMW Explained
with example

SAP PM T-Codes

PM BRD/COR
Maintenance

Add Your URL

User Exits &
Enhancements

Best Of SAP Links

BDC Code

My Resume

SAP ALE and IDOC Transactions .

IDOC / ALE Transactions   IDOC Status Code

SALE   Area Menu for ALE configurations.It
Logical System definition and linking
RFC Destination and Port Definition E

SM59   RFC Destination

Here we specify the login settings for the destination including
the I.P address or Application Server name and the User name and
password. The information entered here is used to run Remote Function
Calls(RFC) on the destination server . We can create number of types
of RFC Destinations but 3 types are important .
R/3 (R/3 to R/3) ,S(logical system) and TCP/IP

WE21 Port Definition. There are 6 types of ports but only 2 types File and Transactional RFC types of ports are important. We have to specify the RFC Destination before a port can be created.

WE57 This is used to assign the Inbound function module to the Message Type and to the IDOC Type.

WE42 This is used to define the process Code for Inbound Processing.

BD95 Define Filter object type . We can specify the field and the table it belongs to as a filter object .

BD59 Assignment of Filter object type to the Message Type . Here we create the link between Filter object and the segment and the message type and the segment Field.

BD50 Set message Type to reducible.

BD65 Define Mandatory Fields.

BD64 Distribution Model. Also known as Customer Distribution Model Used to define all the messages that will be exchanged between remote systems and the name of thes logical systems. Any filters can also be specified. The model once created has to be distributed on every system which will be communicating ,It can be maintained on only One system.

BD21 Creating IDOCs from change pointers. This can be used to create IDOCs from change pointers for a particular message LIKE MATMAS.

BD22 This can be used to delete change pointers.

BD87 Status Monitor. Idocs can be selected base on number of criteria ard there and some continued to have errors. In this situation, you have to correct the system configuration and then reprocess the IDocs again.

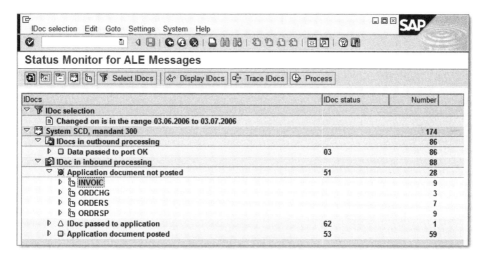

Figure 4.6 Transaction BD87—List of Non-Posted IDocs

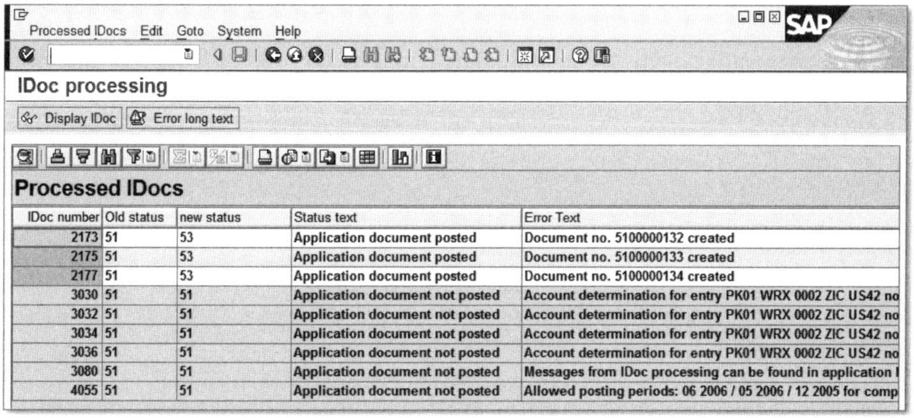

Figure 4.7 Transaction BD87—Result of Reprocessing

4.2.2 Outbound Documents

In some cases, outgoing IDoc messages can also result in errors. The problem usually occurs while leaving the port (described in Chapter 1). There could be a number of reasons; for example, the receiving system may not be available.

1. If reprocessing of the outbound document was not carried out automatically, it can be performed by double-clicking on IDOC ENTRIES IN TRFC QUEUE (see Figure 4.8).

IDocs	IDoc status	Number
▽ 📎 IDoc selection		
📄 Changed on is in the range 03.06.2006 to 03.07.2006		
▽ 🗂 IDES ALE Central system (client 800)		1522
▽ 📄 IDocs in outbound processing		494
🔘 IDoc entries in tRFC queue		299
▷ 📄 Data passed to port OK	03	195
▽ 📄 IDoc in inbound processing		1028

Figure 4.8 Transaction BD87 — Outgoing Documents

2. Select the group of messages of the same message type and click DISPLAY TRFC CALLS. You should see a list of all messages that were not sent.

3. Finally, select the IDocs one by one and select EXECUTE LUW (F6) from the menu. This action will send the IDocs to the external system.

You now know how to handle certain error situations. For incoming IDocs, this involves changing the configuration settings or basic data, and reprocessing of the IDocs.

On the development system, this process can be insufficient and you might have to manually change the IDoc data to process it correctly. This technique is described in the next section.

4.3 IDoc Editing

You can manually change an IDoc and execute it repeatedly. However, this should not be done in a production environment because it would modify the original meaning of the message (for example, the amount to pay).

To change an existing IDoc, you can use the standard Transactions WE02 or WE19. In Transaction WE02, double-click the PAGE icon next to the segment you want to change (see Figure 4.9) and then select DATA RECORD • DISPLAY • CHANGE from the menu. You can then enter values into the segment's fields (see Figure 4.10).

The changes become final after clicking the SAVE icon.

IDoc display
IDoc 0000000000704751
Control Rec.
Data records
Total number: 00000
E1LFA1M
Segment 000001
E1LFBKM
Segment 000002
Status records

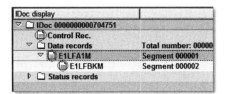

Figure 4.9 Transaction WE02—Segment Icon

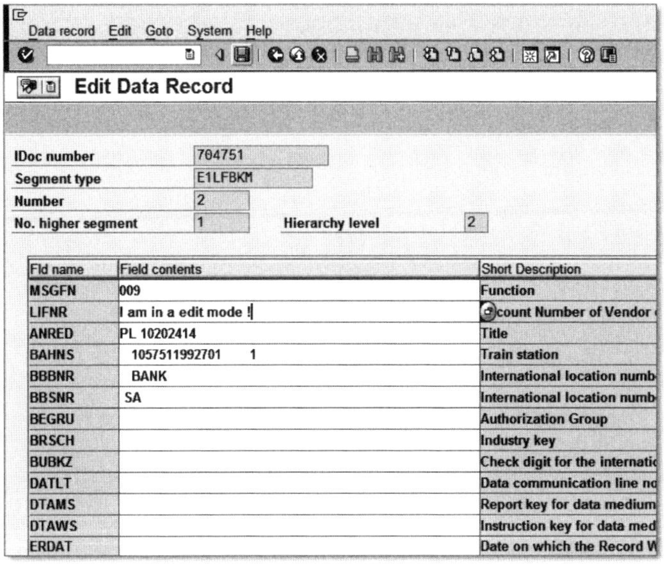

Data record Edit Goto System Help
Edit Data Record
IDoc number
704751
Segment type
E1LFBKM
Number
2
No. higher segment
1
Hierarchy level
2
Fld name
Field contents
Short Description
MSGFN
009
Function
LIFNR
I am in a edit mode !
count Number of Vendor
ANRED
PL 10202414
Title
BAHNS
1057511992701 1
Train station
BBBNR
BANK
International location numb
BBSNR
SA
International location numb
BEGRU
Authorization Group
BRSCH
Industry key
BUBKZ
Check digit for the internati
DATLT
Data communication line no
DTAMS
Report key for data medium
DTAWS
Instruction key for data med
ERDAT
Date on which the Record W

Figure 4.10 Transaction WE02—Editing IDoc

After this step, a copy of the original IDoc is created with status *70: Original of an IDoc that was edited*. The actual IDoc will have status *69: IDoc was edited*. You can process these IDocs in Transaction BD87, just as you did with IDocs that did not post successfully as a result of errors.

4.4 Automated IDoc Monitoring

Monitoring IDoc scenarios can be automated in several (standard) ways. One of them is carried out via business process monitoring using SAP Solution Manager. SAP Solution Manager is a tool used to support companies throughout the entire lifecycle of their SAP solutions and one of the key functionalities it supports—aside from Customizing synchronization, e-learning management, change management, and service desk—is solution monitoring. Solution monitoring allows you to monitor all configured systems at both the system and business process levels. Using alerts, it can notify administrators about even the smallest issues in a system's behavior that can occur during a normal workday, such as too much time used for IDoc processing or too many IDocs with a yellow (processing) status. Even though many sophisticated monitoring solutions can only be implemented using SAP Solution Manager some can also be configured using only the Computing Center Management System (CCMS), which exists in every SAP application system. The next sections will show you how to configure IDoc monitoring in two ways: using CCMS only and using SAP Solution Manager.

4.5   Automated IDoc Monitoring with CCMS

Automated interface monitoring functionalities are based on CCMS. They do not have to be used with SAP Solution Manager; they can also be used as a standalone set of tools. A number of CCMS monitoring templates are available in every SAP application system and can be accessed using Transaction RZ20. One the of monitoring templates called ALE/EDI (see Figure 4.11) allows you to monitor all IDoc message types in both directions (inbound and outbound) and can be accessed directly using Transaction BDMONIC3.

This monitor is an SAP standard monitor and—as mentioned—monitors all IDoc types. It also lets you create a new monitor that will only check the status of specific IDoc message types. Imagine that the sales order creation process is the most important process of a company. Sales orders that arrive from an EDI broker/provider as IDocs sometimes produce an error and cannot be created, mainly because some of the master data is missing. Therefore, the company decides to customize a new CCMS monitor that only monitors the status of sales order IDocs. You can create new monitoring objects for ALE/EDI in Transaction BDMO in a few steps, as follows:

1. Click the CREATE/ACTIVATE MONITORING OBJECTS button on the first screen of Transaction BDMO, as shown in Figure 4.12.

2. In the next step, you need to fill out the new object's name and set its status to ACTIVE, as shown in Figure 4.13.

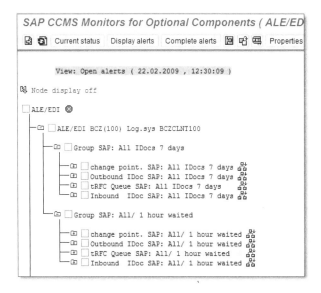

Figure 4.11 Standard ALE/EDI Monitoring Template

Figure 4.12 Creating a New Monitoring Object for ALE/EDI Scenarios

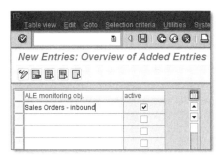

Figure 4.13 Creating an Active ALE/EDI Monitoring Object

3. Next, select the ALE/EDI parameters that will identify the desired monitoring object.

4. Save your monitoring object and open Transaction BDMO once more.

5. When you now click the CHANGE MONITORING OBJECT button (after selecting the new monitoring object), as shown in Figure 4.14, you will see a new screen (Figure 4.15) where you can select the requested parameters.

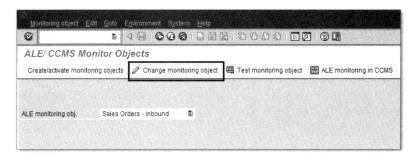

Figure 4.14 Changing the ALE/EDI Monitoring Object

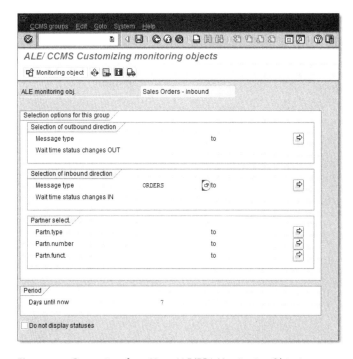

Figure 4.15 Parameters for a New ALE/EDI Monitoring Object

6. Because you only need to monitor one type of IDoc—sales orders—you only need to fill the SELECTION OF INBOUND DIRECTION section with the MESSAGE TYPE parameter. The message type for inbound sales orders is ORDERS. Therefore, fill out this parameter as also shown in Figure 4.15.

7. The WAIT TIME STATUS CHANGES parameters specify the time the system waits to change the status. You use these parameters (both OUT and IN) if an IDoc changes its status less frequently (processing time takes a few minutes for example) and the old status is shown in monitoring. Only when the time specified in the WAIT TIME STATUS CHANGES parameter has passed, will the monitoring receive the information about the new status.

8. The PARTNER SELECT section is fairly self explanatory. It allows you to specify from which partner (in case of inbound IDocs) or to which partner (in case of outbound IDocs) the message will be delivered. Remember that monitoring objects are transportable objects, which means that if you want to specify the transmission partner, you must use the same partner number you will use on production system. However, selecting a partner from the production system is only possible if you create the partners in the development system.

9. The last parameter you can specify is DAYS UNTIL NOW. With this parameter you can set up—in days—the age of IDocs whose status will be checked by this monitoring object. If the IDoc is older than what is specified in the DAYS UNTIL NOW parameter, it will not be taken into consideration.

10. After you save the configured monitoring object you need to start it. This can be done in the starting screen of Transaction BDMO by selecting the START ALL option from the menu, as shown in Figure 4.16.

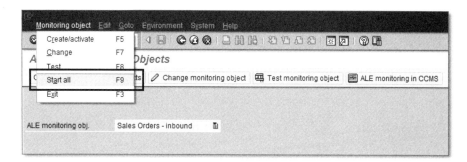

Figure 4.16 Starting Data Collection for the Monitoring Object

11. This will start the collection only once. To schedule a collection, you need to use Transaction RZ21 and select TECHNICAL INFRASTRUCTURE • METHOD EXECUTION • ACTIVATE BACKGROUND DISPATCHING, as shown in Figure 4.17.

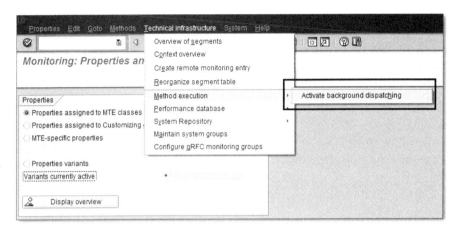

Figure 4.17 Scheduling Data Collection for Monitoring Objects

When you open Transaction BDMONIC3, you should be able to see a new monitor (node) called GROUP SALES ORDERS – INBOUND. This is the newly created monitoring object. If any IDocs are running already, you should be able to see them. In this case, as you can see from Figure 4.18, there are eight IDocs with an application error under the GROUP SALES ORDERS – INBOUND node. This means they need to be checked because something is wrong.

Node colors (green, yellow, and red) can be customized per node. When you select the node INBOUND: ERROR IN APPLICATION and click ⇧+F7 (*Properties*) you will see a screen as shown in Figure 4.19. The most important values you can set here are the THRESHOLD VALUES. Threshold values specify the number of IDocs available in each node under which the status of the node changes. For example, Figure 4.19 shows that when there are more than six IDocs in the node INBOUND: ERROR IN APPLICATION, the node status will change to red.

If you want to analyze errors shown in different nodes, you only need to double-click on the node. This will take you directly to Transaction WE02, where you can check the error details. With this new monitoring object, our sample company can monitor a single type of IDocs—sales orders—which was the business requirement in this case.

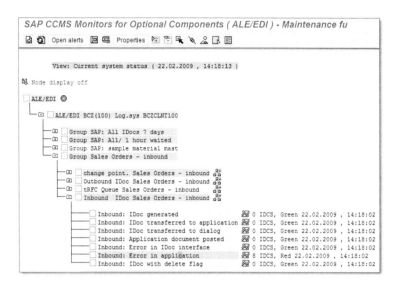

Figure 4.18 New Monitoring Object in Transaction BDMONIC3

Monitoring: Properties and Methods

| Properties of | BCZ\ALE/EDI BCZ(100) Log.sys BCZCLNT100\...\Inbound IDoc Sales Orders - inb... |
| MTE class | ALEIDcMTAttCl |

General | PerformanceAttribute | Methods | Addtl info

Performance properties assigned from group   ALEPfGr:Sales Orders - inbouF

Comparative value
- ● Last reported value
- ○ Average in the last hour
- ○ Average in the last quarter of an hour
- ○ Smoothing over last 1 min.
- ○ Smoothing over last 5 min.
- ○ Smoothing over last 15 mins

Threshold values

Change from GREEN to YELLOW	3	IDCS
Change from YELLOW to RED	6	IDCS
Reset from RED to YELLOW	5	IDCS
Reset from YELLOW to GREEN	2	IDCS

Alert is triggered if the comparative value
- ○ falls below threshold value
- ● exceeds the threshold value

Alert text

Message class	B1
Message number	626
Text	&1 IDocs for this monitoring object found but threshold value is &2

Reorganization schema for the performance DB

Figure 4.19 Changing Threshold Values for CCMS Monitoring Nodes

4.6   IDoc Monitoring with Solution Manager

If there is more than one SAP application system (ERP, CRM, SRM, etc.) in a company, monitoring IDocs on each of them can be a very difficult task, for several reasons:

▶ If you monitor the IDocs on each of the SAP application systems, you need to log on to them each time you receive an alert and want to check the reason for the alert.

▶ If you monitor the IDocs on each of the systems you may not know the business processes affected by the interfaces.

The first reason should be clear; that is why we will concentrate only on the second one for now. Many companies use a variety of systems in their landscape and all of those systems perform different roles. Imagine you need to send out sales orders from an SAP ERP system to another planning system that checks material availability before delivery creation. If the planning system does not receive any messages, the people responsible for managing the system may not know why this is happening because there could be many reasons: there may not be any sales orders inside SAP ERP that need to be checked, some sales orders may not be in a status that requires sending the message to the planning system yet, or all sales orders may already be distributed to the planning system but did not reach the system for some reason. If, in addition, these sales orders can arrive from several ERP systems, checking what is wrong by calling the responsible persons would be a very long and cumbersome task.

On the other hand, imagine that you have one system in which you can create a business process for sales order distribution and link this process to all application systems that take part in it. This way, if you want to check errors for the entire business process, you only have to look at one system.

SAP Solution Manager is a tool that can easily act as such a consolidation system for business process monitoring. In the next section, we will describe how to configure a sample business process with one IDoc interface and how monitoring of interfaces in this business process can be done afterwards. There are a number of steps and prerequisites that need to be fulfilled to configure SAP Solution Manager for business process monitoring, including the following:

▶ All SAP application systems (such as ERP, CRM, and SRM) must have the ST-PI and ST-A/PI plug-ins installed.

- Solution Manager must have all of your SAP application systems configured with RFC connectivity to those systems.
- A solution needs to be created in which you will configure business processes.

Because these items are usually maintained by the Basis team, we will not describe them in detail here. There are also a number of steps you need to carry out in SAP Solution Manager to set up business process monitoring functionality, as follows:

- Create a business process that will represent the sample process: sending sales order IDocs.
- Create an interface scenario you will append to the business process created in the first step.
- Configure the interface scenario monitoring to check only for errors that occur in the sample monitoring object—sales order inbound—created in Section 4.5.

After you complete these steps, you will be ready to perform a sample monitoring of the business process.

4.6.1   Creating a Business Process

First, you need to create a business process you will be monitoring to see if there are any IDocs with error statuses. One of the prerequisites for this is a new solution (a basic element in which you can create your objects) inside SAP Solution Manager. In our example, the name of the solution is "demo krawczyk" (as you can see in the SOLUTION STRUCTURE in Figure 4.20).

Figure 4.20 Business Process Creation

1. When you open the solution, you first need to create a business scenario. You do this in the BUSINESS SCENARIOS node. Select the node, enter the name "DEMO BOOK" into the SCENARIO field and save it.

2. After you saved the scenario, a several nodes appear. One of them will be the BUSINESS PROCESSES node. After you open this node, you can enter a sample business process such as DEMOPROCESS, as shown in Figure 4.20.

3. After you have saved the new business process, you should see it in the SOLUTION STRUCTURE area of the screen. Expand the process to be able to add steps to it.

4. As shown in Figure 4.21, you will add just two steps—IDOC SEND and IDOC RECEIVE. Both will use the same logical component (the same SAP application systems). Because this is a demo, you only configured one SAP application system (step 2 of the prerequisites). This system will be used as both sender and receiver of the messages.

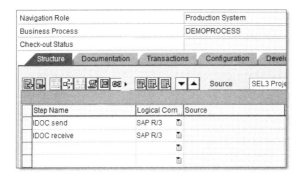

Figure 4.21 Multiple Step Business Process Creation with Logical System Assignment

After you save the solution, the demo business process is ready to be used. Next, you need to add an interface between the two steps. However, this can only be done after a new interface scenario is available.

4.6.2 Interface Scenario Creation

After the business scenario has been created, you need to create an interface scenario object that will tell the system which components take part in the process. Proceed as follows:

1. As shown in Figure 4.22, select the INTERFACE SCENARIOS node and enter "IDOC" as the interface scenario's description.

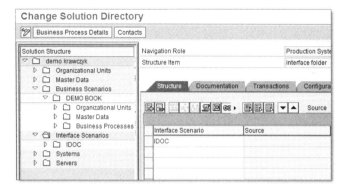

Figure 4.22 Interface Scenario Creation

2. After you have saved the new interface scenario, you should see it in the SOLUTION STRUCTURE area of the screen. Expand it to be able to add interfaces to the sample interface scenario. As shown in Figure 4.23, you will add one interface—IDOC SEND. You need to fill out the fields SENDING LOGICAL SYSTEM and RECEIVING LOGICAL SYSTEM (which in our case will be the same system as explained in Section 4.6.1). You also need to add the TECHNOLOGY used—ALE (for IDocs)—and the TYPE—2 ASYNCHRONOUS (because IDocs are always asynchronous messages).

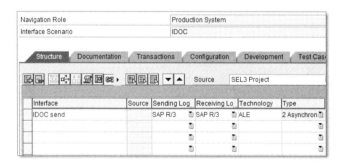

Figure 4.23 Interface Creation with Logical Systems and Technology Assignment

3. After you have created an interface, you can add steps for the interface by selecting the IDOC SEND scenario in the SOLUTION STRUCTURE in the left area of

the screen. Add an interface step—SENDIDOC—together with a LOGICAL COM-PONENT (the same one used for the interface definition), as shown in Figure 4.24.

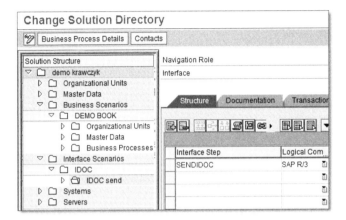

Figure 4.24 Interface Step Definition

4. When the interface is ready, go back to the business process you created in Section 4.6.1 and select the GRAPHICAL VIEW tab. This view will show the graphical definition of the business process with both of the steps you configured. From this view, you need to append an interface between the two steps. You can do so by right-clicking on both interfaces and selecting CREATE LINE (ASYNCHRONOUSLY) from the menu, as shown in Figure 4.25.

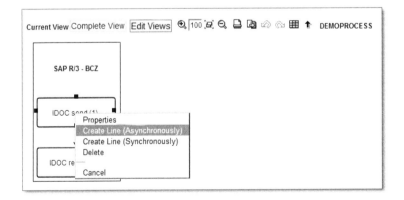

Figure 4.25 Adding an Interface Between two Business Process Steps—Part 1

5. After the line connects the two business process steps, you need to right-click on this new line and select ASSIGN INTERFACE from the menu, as shown in Figure 4.26.

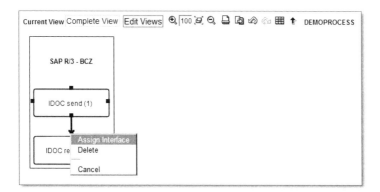

Figure 4.26 Adding an Interface Between Two Business Process Steps—Part 2

6. A new pop-up window appears where you will be able to select the IDOC SEND interface, as shown in Figure 4.27.

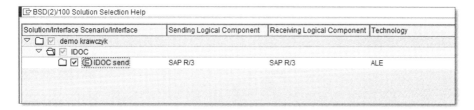

Figure 4.27 Selecting an Interface for the Interface to Business Process assignment

This portion of the configuration is now complete and you now have a business process with an interface defined. The only thing left to do is assigning the monitoring applications (e.g., ALE monitoring objects) that will be used for business process monitoring.

4.6.3 Configuring Interface Scenario Monitoring

To add the new ALE monitoring object created in Section 4.5, you need to use the BACK button on the main solution screen and select OPERATIONS • BUSINESS PROCESS MONITORING • SETUP BUSINESS PROCESS MONITORING.

1. This opens the BUSINESS PROCESS MONITORING screen. Here, under the BUSI-
   NESS PROCESSES node, you need to select the checkbox in the SELECT column, as
   shown in Figure 4.28.

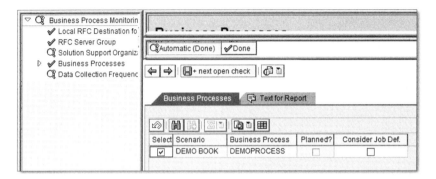

Figure 4.28 Selecting A Scenario for Monitoring

2. After you have saved the selection, the node will be created with the same
   name as your business process. You then need to select the INTERFACE MONI-
   TORING node and again select the checkbox in the SELECT column next to the
   INTERFACE name, as shown in Figure 4.29.

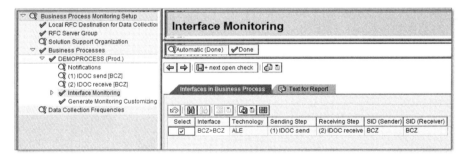

Figure 4.29 Selecting the Interface for Monitoring

3. When you save the new selection again, a new node appears (Figure 4.30).
   From there, you need to select the checkbox next to the INTERFACE MONITORING
   (CCMS) row because you will be using the custom monitoring object created in
   Transaction BDMO.

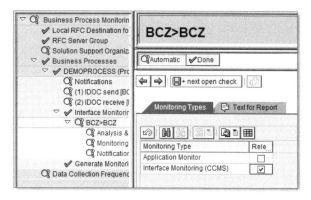

Figure 4.30 CCMS Monitoring Selection

4. After you have saved the entry, a new node appears under the node with your interface's name called INTERFACE MONITORING (CCMS). If you open this node, you need to click on the RELOAD CCMS: ALE MON OBJECTS button shown in Figure 4.31.

5. When you press F4 on the SID column, a new search help box will appear with the same custom monitoring objects from the SAP application system created in Transaction BDMO (see Figure 4.31).

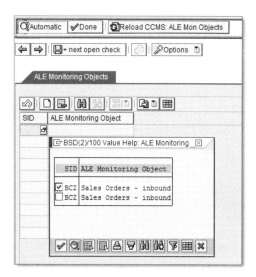

Figure 4.31 Selecting a Monitoring Object

6. Select any of the monitoring objects (you can see two objects because you are using the same system for the sender and the receiver) and save the entry.

7. Again, after you have saved the entry, a new node appears called ALERT MONITORS. When you open this node, you need to perform a sequence of steps. All of them are shown in Figure 4.32:

   ▷ Click the RELEASE CCMS: THRESHOLDS button to get the threshold values from the ERP system on which you configured Transaction BDMO.

   ▷ Click the COPY ALL button to copy the thresholds.

   ▷ Select the ALE monitoring alerts you want to use. We suggest that you select at least the following alert: BCZ: SALES ORDERS – INBOUND/INBOUND: ERROR IN APPLICATION.

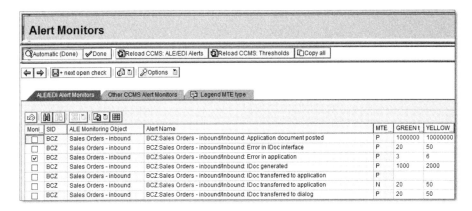

Figure 4.32 Alert Selection for Monitoring Objects

8. You now need to go to the GENERATE MONITORING node and click the GENERATE+ACTIVATE MONITORING button, as shown in Figure 4.33.

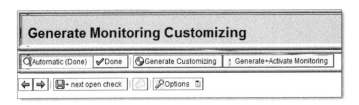

Figure 4.33 Activating Monitoring

9. If the activation was successful and there are no errors in the log on the activation screen, you can proceed to the next steps. If there are errors, we suggest checking whether all of the steps were performed as shown. If the error persists, you may need to check the OSS notes because the issue may not be related to Customizing.

10. After you are done with the monitoring Customizing, you can check whether errors are visible in SAP Solution Manager. To do so, you need to go back (press [F3]) from the business process monitoring setup and click on the OP-ERATIONS link.

11. You should then see a screen, as shown in Figure 4.34, with the DEMOPROCESS scenarioobject. You can click on this to check its details.

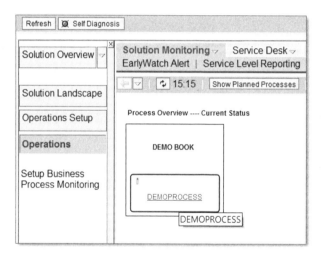

Figure 4.34 Process Overview General Screen

12. When you are in the details view for the process, you can see the interface represented as a line from one process step (send) to another (receive), with a DISPLAY ALERTS icon, as shown in Figure 4.35.

13. When you click on the DISPLAY ALERTS icon, you will see all alerts generated by the custom ALE monitoring object created with Transaction BDMO, as shown in Figure 4.36.

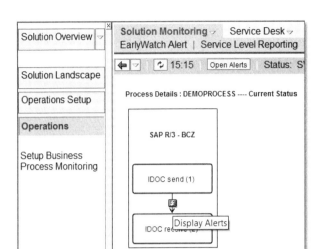

Figure 4.35 Process Details Screen

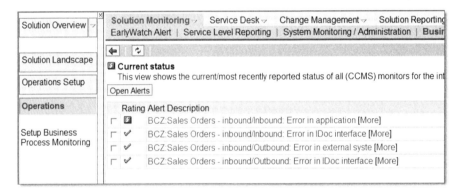

Figure 4.36 ALE Alerts for a Custom Monitoring Object

14. When you doubleclick on an alert, it will take you to a screen from where you can use all standard transactions for IDOC monitoring such as Transaction BD87 (for IDoc reprocessing) or Transaction WE05 (for IDoc monitoring).

15. When you open any of these transactions, they will redirect you directly to the monitored system, which was the goal of this exercise.

The solution shown in this chapter allows you to monitor not only all SAP application systems in one place but most important, it allows you to monitor business processes that are happening across these systems. All IDoc interfaces used in these business processes can be easily monitored in a single place. This can not only speed up solving issues related to any of the interfaces but will also show you which business processes are directly affected so that the business can also react.

4.7   Summary

This chapter explained how to monitor for and handle potential IDoc problems in the SAP application system. In most cases, however, this is not the only administrative work that has to be done. IDocs can also cause errors in middleware software such as SAP NetWeaver PI. IDoc monitoring from the SAP NetWeaver PI side will be described in the next chapter.

5 SAP NetWeaver PI in IDoc Scenarios

This chapter provides you with an overview of SAP NetWeaver PI, as well as the technical steps you need to perform to use SAP NetWeaver PI to transfer IDocs.

5.1 SAP NetWeaver PI Introduction

SAP NetWeaver PI enables you to connect with all systems that support IDoc information exchange. Essentially, SAP NetWeaver PI is a process-integration tool that can integrate one or many business systems. We can distinguish two types of activities supported by SAP NetWeaver PI:

▸ **Cross-system application integration**
This is responsible for the runtime part of integration flows, and no user action is required.

▸ **Administration and development**
This focuses on the development of new as well as the administration of existing integration flows.

Both types of activities will be presented in the next sections regarding IDoc message exchange.

Design of SAP NetWeaver PI

SAP NetWeaver PI consists of three main parts, as shown in Figure 5.1:

▸ Integration Builder

▸ Integration Server

▸ System Landscape Directory (SLD)

The *Integration Builder* serves as the main tool for modeling new integration flows. It consists of the Integration Repository and the Integration Directory. The *Integration Repository* is used for building all objects that will become relevant for transport. This includes data types, message interfaces, message mappings, and integration scenarios. You can see the most important repository objects in Figure 5.2.

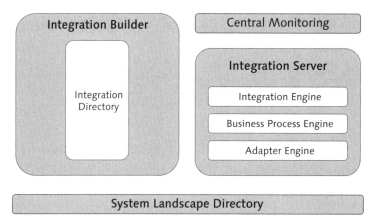

Figure 5.1 SAP NetWeaver PI Schema

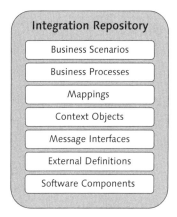

Figure 5.2 Integration Repository Objects

The *Integration Directory*, on the other hand, is maintained separately for every landscape. What you transport are only routing conditions. The system names can differ from one landscape to another, for example, during transport from development systems to quality assurance systems. Figure 5.3 shows the most important Integration Directory objects.

Communication channels are among the objects maintained in the Integration Directory. These are based on *adapters*. Adapters are services used to communicate with systems that can use messages structures other than the XML messages supported by SAP NetWeaver PI, or that use different protocols to communicate. In the next sections, one of these adapters—the IDoc adapter—and the communication using this adapter will be discussed in detail.

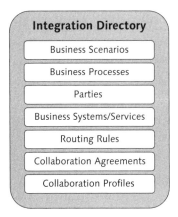

Figure 5.3 Integration Directory Objects

The *Integration Server* is the SAP NetWeaver PI runtime component responsible for receiving incoming messages and controlling how these messages are forwarded to receiver systems. It consists of three parts:

▶ **Integration Engine**
The Integration Engine is the runtime environment of SAP NetWeaver PI.

▶ **Business Process Engine**
The Business Process Engine controls how all of the steps of the integration process are defined and executed during runtime.

▶ **Adapter Engine**
The Adapter Engine is used to connect with external systems.

The third part of the SAP NetWeaver PI design is the *SLD* (see Figure 5.4), which is the central location where information about the entire landscape is maintained. It contains two types of information:

▶ **Landscape description**
The landscape description contains a list of all installed systems in the landscape, both technical and business systems.

▶ **Component information**
Component information contains information about products and components of different systems. These are maintained in the Software Catalog.

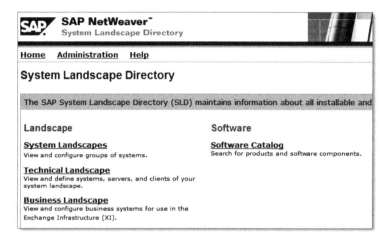

Figure 5.4 SLD

All components of SAP NetWeaver PI and all of the flows that run through it can be centrally monitored by a component called *Runtime Workbench* (RWB). It consists of several monitors that can be used on IDoc exchange flows from different angles:

▶ **Component monitoring**
Component monitoring allows you to check the status of every SAP NetWeaver PI component (Integration Engine, adapters, etc.).

▶ **Message monitoring**
With message monitoring, you can monitor messages that flow through the Integration Engine, in a way that is similar to using Transaction SXMB_MONI.

▶ **End-to-end monitoring**
Using End-to-end monitoring, you can check which components were involved in a particular flow.

▶ **Performance monitoring**
Performance monitoring allows you to check the speed of different flows, based on many selection and grouping criteria.

▶ **Index administration**
Index administration is used to start or stop message indexing (messages can be indexed via the TREX engine).

▶ **Alert configuration**
The alert configuration is used to maintain alerts that later can be called from the integration flows and passed to an email account or a short message service (SMS).

▶ **Cache monitoring**
Cache monitoring lets you monitor the content of the cache currently in use.

Not all of these monitors, such as index administration, need to be configured and used but it is always good to know in which situations they can help you with which type of issues.

5.2   IDoc Exchange Basics Using SAP NetWeaver PI

SAP NetWeaver PI enables you to connect with systems that support IDoc information exchange. Although only IDocs from SAP systems Release 3.1x or higher are supported, you can also send IDoc messages from an external (third-party) system to the Integration Server, SAP NetWeaver PI's core engine.

The Integration Server can communicate with different systems through the *IDoc adapter*. You can use the IDoc adapter in all integration scenarios as long as message flow is asynchronous and one of the involved systems can process IDocs. IDoc exchange cannot be carried out synchronously. In most cases—other than in IDoc tunneling, which will be discussed later—IDocs inside the Integration Server are transformed into XML messages called *IDOC-XML*. In a manner of speaking, IDOC-XML is just an XML representation of the IDoc.

In Listing 5.1, you can see an example of the MBGMCR02 IDoc in XML format. As you can see, it has the same segment names as standard IDoc MBGMCR02.

```xml
<?xml version="1.0" encoding="UTF-8"?>
<MBGMCR02>
   <IDOC BEGIN="">
      <E1MBGMCR SEGMENT="">
         <TESTRUN/>
      </E1MBGMCR>
      <E1BP2017_GM_HEAD_01 SEGMENT="">
         <PSTNG_DATE>01012010</PSTNG_DATE>
         <DOC_DATE>01012010</DOC_DATE>
         <REF_DOC_NO>43234566666</REF_DOC_NO>
```

```
          <BILL_OF_LADING/>
          <GR_GI_SLIP_NO/>
          <PR_UNAME/>
          <HEADER_TXT/>
          <EXT_WMS/>
          <REF_DOC_NO_LONG/>
          <BILL_OF_LADING_LONG/>
          <BAR_CODE/>
      </E1BP2017_GM_HEAD_01>
      <E1BP2017_GM_ITEM_CREATE SEGMENT="">
          <MATERIAL/>
          <PLANT/>
        ✗ <STGE_LOC/>        S- O C.
          <BATCH/>
          <MOVE_TYPE/>
          <STCK_TYPE/>
          <SPEC_STOCK/>
    </IDOC>
</MBGMCR02>
```

Listing 5.1 MBGMCR02 IDoc in the XML Format

IDoc adapter configuration is different for the inbound channel (when IDocs are being sent to SAP NetWeaver PI) than it is for the outbound channel (when IDocs are being sent from SAP NetWeaver PI). The message exchanges between IDoc sender and IDoc receiver systems are very similar, however. The two adapters involved are as follows:

▸ **IDoc sender adapter**
This adapter is used to send messages to the Integration Engine. When you send IDocs to SAP NetWeaver PI, they are processed by this service on the Integration Engine unless an IDoc message is included in an exception table (see Section 5.12).

▸ **IDoc receiver adapter**
This adapter is used to send messages from the Integration Engine. It is called after all services inside the Integration Engine process the IDOC-XML. The adapter then transforms the IDOC-XML into a standard IDoc format and sends it through the IDoc RFC interface.

5.2.1   IDoc Metadata Inside the Integration Repository and Integration Engine

To process an IDoc in the form of an IDOC-XML message, an IDoc's metadata must be loaded into the Integration Server so that SAP NetWeaver PI's IDoc adapter can change the native IDoc format into the XML representation. This metadata is simply a description of available structures and fields and can be loaded in two ways:

▶ During runtime
▶ Before the actual message flow ↦ ~~Prefers~~ -

The second method, uploading the metadata before running integration scenarios, is advisable because you can be sure that the IDoc definitions are those you really want, given that the IDoc's metadata is visible right after the import. If the system does not allow exporting the metadata (as is the case with some third-party systems), you can reference an SAP system as your metadata repository. If problems occur, you can take a look at your metadata description with Transaction IDX2, which is used to upload or check metadata.

In Figure 5.5, you can see an example of an IDoc's metadata description, uploaded from an SAP system via Transaction IDX2. To see the description, you need to double-click the IDoc's name. As you can see, it contains field descriptions very similar to a standard IDoc description taken from Transaction WE60.

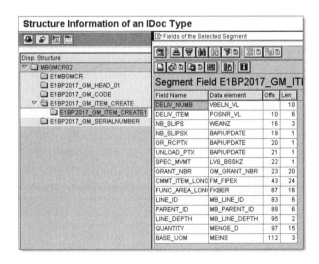

IDX2 – METADATA

Figure 5.5 IDoc Metadata

5.2.2 IDoc Metadata Comparison

As of service pack 08 for SAP NetWeaver PI 7.0 (SP17 for XI 3.0), a new report exists called `IDX_CHECK_METADATA`. This report lets you compare a system's current metadata with a reference system. This function can be very useful in the development system, where you often change the structures of customer IDocs while developing the integration scenario.

After the metadata is loaded into the system (as described earlier in this section), it is not loaded again during every call. This is why any changes in the IDoc's structure would not be reflected in the new flow.

The new report `IDX_CHECK_METADATA` helps to quickly check whether the data needs to be reloaded. You can start the report from Transaction SE38. After the report starts, you need to fill at least two fields (see Figure 5.6), as follows:

▶ **Port**
In this field, you have to enter the port from Transaction IDX1 from which you want to compare the IDoc's metadata.

▶ **Basic Type**
In this field, you have to fill out the IDoc's basic type name.

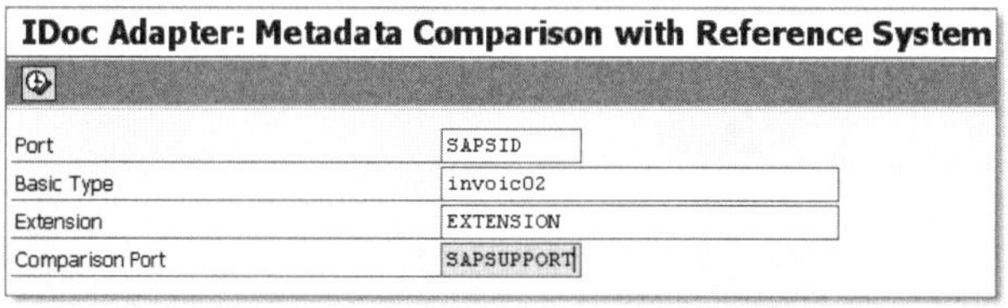

Figure 5.6 Report IDX_CHECK_METADATA

If you are using an IDoc's extension, you can also put its name in the report (field EXTENSION). Clicking the EXECUTE button will cause the metadata to be downloaded from the IDoc port and compared with the existing metadata. You can see an example of this comparison in Figure 5.7.

Figure 5.7 shows that there are three types of statuses you can see in this report, as follows:

▶ **Icon with a plus sign**
When you see this icon, it means that the remote system (the one you want to compare) has more fields than the IDoc's metadata loaded to SAP NetWeaver PI.

▸ **Icon with a minus sign**
When you see this icon, it means that the IDoc from the remote system has been reduced, and that there are more fields in SAP NetWeaver PI's cache.

▸ **Icon with a pencil**
This icon means that the segment names are the same but the structures are different (offsets, or lengths).

IDoc Adapter: Metadata Comparison with Reference System

Port: SAP
Basic Type/Ext. INVOIC02 /ZINV05
No. of Differences: 19

StatusGr	Segment type	Field Name	Offset	Export length	Segm.type	Remote Fld Name	Offset	Length
								4
							4	10
							14	20
							34	1
							35	3
							38	8
							46	8
							54	8
							62	30

Figure 5.7 Metadata Comparison

If you see any of these three types of inconsistencies in this report, you can delete the metadata from the specified port directly by clicking the DELETE button. The new metadata will be reloaded during the next flow, or you can import it manually, as shown earlier in this section. If your SAP NetWeaver PI system version is lower than service pack 17, you can delete the IDoc's metadata directly by using Transaction IDX2 or by using an older report (IDX_RESET_METADATA). Keep in mind, however, that these two alternative methods will not tell you whether you need to reload because they do not compare anything.

The information from this section should give you an idea of how the IDoc messages look from SAP NetWeaver PI's perspective. In the next section, we will concentrate on the configuration of the IDoc flows.

5.3 Sending IDocs to SAP NetWeaver PI

To start sending IDocs to SAP NetWeaver PI from an SAP application system (SAP R/3, SAP ECC, etc.), you have to configure both ends: the SAP application system and SAP NetWeaver PI. In this section, we will not discuss how to send IDocs—using partner profiles, Message Control, or logical system creation—from the SAP application system side. This process was described in Chapter 1, and the configuration is exactly the same in this situation.

5.3.1 SAP Application System Configuration

The only difference is the creation of an RFC destination via Transaction SM59, as follows:

1. Start Transaction SM59 in your SAP application system.

2. Specify CONNECTION TYPE 3 (R/3 CONNECTION) for the RFC Connection and provide the TARGET HOST and SYSTEM NUMBER to your SAP NetWeaver PI system (see Figure 5.8). This information can be found in the SAPLOGON • PROPERTIES menu (right-click the SAP instance entry).

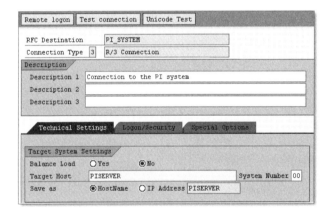

Figure 5.8 RFC Destination to SAP NetWeaver PI

3. You also have to add a user name and a password on the LOGON/SECURITY tab.

4. In most cases, you will be using partner type LS LOGICAL SYSTEM when sending data to the NetWeaver PI system. Therefore, configuration on the SAP application system is done for now.

The next thing you have to do is add your SAP application system to the SLD: the place where all systems' descriptions are kept. You can do this manually by creating the entry in the SLD or automatically by using a special transaction (Transaction RZ70), which will be described later. You have to add two objects:

▶ **Technical system**

This is the hardware system, which in our case will be an SAP server.

▶ **Business system**

This resides on a technical system but is regarded more as a logical sender/ receiver. In SAP systems, it represents a client.

The easiest way to add an SAP application system to the SLD is by using standard Transaction RZ70 on your SAP application system (see Figure 5.9). Proceed as follows:

1. Specify the GATEWAY INFORMATION about the SLD BRIDGE, entered in the fields HOST and SERVICE.

2. If your SLD was installed with SAP NetWeaver PI, you have to specify the XI host in the HOST field and the XI gateway in the GATEWAY field and execute the data distribution.

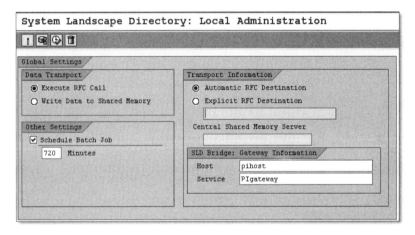

Figure 5.9 Technical System Creation

After you finished registering your SAP application in the SLD, you should be able to see it under the TECHNICAL LANDSCAPE link in the SLD (Transaction SLD-CHECK).

5.3.2   SAP NetWeaver PI Configuration

The next step is to add your application system's client as a business system in the SLD. Proceed as follows:

1. Open the BUSINESS LANDSCAPE with a click on the appropriate link and select NEW BUSINESS SYSTEM.

2. When specifying the business system name, use standard naming convention `<SID>CLNT<client number>`, where `<SID>` stands for the SAP system ID.

3. Next, you have to select the SAP NetWeaver Application Server (AS) ABAP. This means that you want to use this business system to send data from the SAP application server's ABAP engine, given that you want to send IDocs.

4. On the next screen, you have to select the SAP application's technical system, which you previously added using Transaction RZ70. You need to select the client from which you will send messages and an Integration Server with which your business system will communicate.

5. After you are done, you should be able to see a new business system in the business system landscape.[1]

Next, you need to perform the configuration in the Integration Directory, where you specify routing configuration for all of the integration scenarios. To work with an SAP application system, you have to add its business system. Proceed as follows:

1. You can add the business system as a SERVICE WITHOUT PARTY on the OBJECTS tab of the Integration Directory. Here, you have to select ASSIGN BUSINESS SYSTEM... in the context menu (see Figure 5.10).

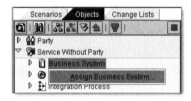

Figure 5.10 Assigning a Business System

2. After you select your business system, you have to remember to check the *adapter-specific identifiers*. Adapter-specific identifiers are used by SAP NetWeaver PI during runtime to map the system's name to a name used by cer-

---

1 If you want your system to be able to connect to SAP NetWeaver PI using ABAP proxy connections, you need a full SLD registration. Check the SAP NetWeaver PI Configuration Guide for details.

tain adapters (e.g., IDoc adapters). This will help avoid a common error, which sends the message that SAP NetWeaver PI cannot convert ALE systems to any party on the NetWeaver PI server.

3. You can check the identifiers by selecting your new business system in the Integration Directory and navigating to SERVICE • ADAPTER SPECIFIC IDENTIFIERS in the main menu of this business system.

4. If you are in change mode of the business system object, you have to use the COMPARE WITH SYSTEM LANDSCAPE DIRECTORY button to check whether the logical system name is correctly filled in the Integration Directory configuration (see Figure 5.11).

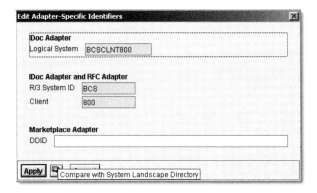

Figure 5.11 Adapter-Specific Identifiers

5. After you apply the logical system name from the SLD, you can save the configuration and activate it on the CHANGE LISTS tab. By doing so, you ensure that all changes will be saved and placed into the appropriate cache.

Next, you also need to perform some configuration actions from the SAP GUI. You must configure two elements, as follows:

► RFC destination to the R/3 or ECC system

► IDoc port

The RFC destination to the R/3 or ECC system is exactly the same as the RFC destination from the R/3 or ECC system to SAP NetWeaver PI. However, you have to point to the SAP R/3 or ECC system instead of SAP NetWeaver PI and use a user that exists on the SAP R/3 or ECC application system.

The IDoc port is required to create an RFC connection with the system that will send messages to SAP NetWeaver PI to supply the IDoc's metadata. This metadata is used later to convert the standard IDoc into its XML representation, which can be used in SAP NetWeaver PI for mappings, routings, and so on. To maintain the IDoc port, proceed as follows:

1. First, make sure that you are using a user with the role SAP_XI_ADMINISTRATOR.

2. Access Transaction IDX1.

3. When creating the IDoc port, you have to enter the following data (see Figure 5.12):

   ▷ **Port**
   This requires the port's name. The name must fulfill the naming convention SAP<SID>, where SID is your SAP R/3 or ECC application system's ID.

   ▷ **Client**
   This is the standard SAP system's client.

   ▷ **RFC Destination**
   This field refers to the previously created RFC destination to the SAP system.

   ▷ **Description**
   This field needs to be filled with a meaningful description of the port.

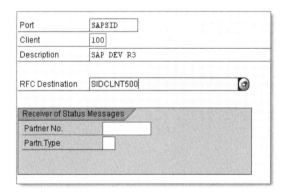

Figure 5.12 IDoc Port on the Integration Server

The IDoc's metadata should be loaded into SAP NetWeaver PI during the first message flow but it is good practice to load the metadata manually to make sure that everything will work correctly. To load the metadata, you need a user with the `SAP_XI_CONFIGURATOR` role. This role enables you to use Transaction IDX2 (see Figure 5.13).

To load a new set of metadata, you have to supply an IDoc Type in the IDoc Type field, as shown in Figure 5.13. This is the IDoc basic type such as `ORDERS04`, `INVOIC02`, or `MATMAS05`. You also have to specify the source port in the Source Port field, which the IDoc port created with Transaction IDX1. As an alternative, you can specify the IDoc's extension, providing that your IDoc was extended with additional segments.

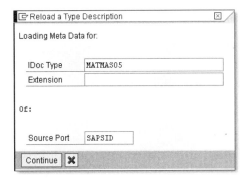

Figure 5.13 Loading Metadata for IDoc MATMAS05

5.3.3 Running a Test procedure for Sending IDocs to SAP NetWeaver PI

When this basic configuration is done, you can perform a simple test. To send a test IDoc to SAP NetWeaver PI, you do not need any objects in the Integration Directory. In particular, you do not need the sender agreement because there is no sender IDoc adapter in the Integration Directory.[2] When your configuration on the SAP application system (R/3 or ECC) is done, you can run the previously mentioned test using Transaction WE19.

1. First, you have to select the IDoc's basic type (BasicTyp) that you want to send for testing. In our case, the IDoc will be of type `RSINFO`, as shown in Figure 5.14.

---

2 Please note that this is the case only with IDoc and HTTP adapters and only until service pack 16. From then on, you need to create a sender agreement to use adapter-specific messaging attributes, for example.

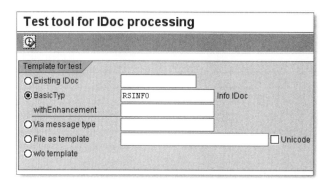

Figure 5.14 IDoc Test Tool

2. Next, to be able to send the IDoc to SAP NetWeaver PI, you need to populate the IDoc control record fields with the following values (see Figure 5.15):

 ‣ **Receiver Partner No.**
   Here, you have to enter the SAP NetWeaver PI's logical system taken from Transaction WE20 (LOGICAL SYSTEMS node).

 ‣ **Receiver Port**
   This is the port pointing to SAP NetWeaver PI. You can get it from Transaction WE21.

 ‣ **Receiver Part. Type**
   Here, you have to enter a constant value. We chose LS because in most cases, you use the logical system as a receiver of IDocs.

 ‣ **Sender Partner No.**
   This information can be taken from Transaction WE20 of the SAP application system (LOGICAL SYSTEMS node). Here, you enter your SAP application's logical system name assigned to the SAP client.

 ‣ **Sender Port**
   SAP<SID>—a virtual port you can use in Transaction WE19.

 ‣ **Sender Part. Type**
   Here, you have to enter a constant value. We chose LS again because in most cases, you use the logical system as the sender of IDocs.

 ‣ **Logical Message Type**
   Here, you have to enter the logical message type you want to send to SAP NetWeaver PI (RSINFO, ORDERS, etc.).

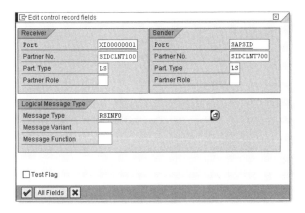

Figure 5.15 IDoc's Control Record

3. Next, you have to fill the IDoc record with dummy values. You can do this by clicking any segment except the control record and filling it with values.

4. Finally, you can generate and send your IDoc using the STANDARD OUTBOUND PROCESSING button. This procedure was described in Chapter 4.

To check whether the IDoc message was delivered to SAP NetWeaver PI, you need to check two things on your SAP application system. These factors are the same as shown in Chapter 4, but here you need to look at them only from the external system's (SAP NetWeaver PI's) point of view:

▶ **Transaction WE02**
Here, you can see whether the IDoc has a green status (*03: IDoc sent to R/3 system or external program*).

▶ **Transaction SM58**
Within this transaction, you can see whether any errors were issued with the transactional RFC (tRFC) call to the external system which in this case, is the SAP NetWeaver PI system, as shown in Figure 5.16.

Transactional RFC

🗑 🔄 Refresh

Caller	Function Module	Target System	Date
Nothing was selected			

Figure 5.16 Transactional RFC Monitor

If there are errors, you need to go back and check the configuration again because something is probably missing. If there are no errors on the application system side, you can check whether the IDoc arrived at SAP NetWeaver PI. Proceed as follows:

1. Go to Transaction SXI_MONITOR, and start it by pressing F8.

2. Here, the IDoc message should look like the one shown in Figure 5.17.

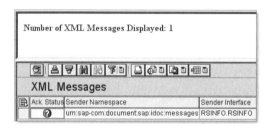

Figure 5.17 An IDoc's Acknowledgment Status

3. The ACK. STATUS column, which stands for *acknowledgment status*, shows the status of the IDoc's acknowledgment. If you see a question mark, this means that the message is waiting for the acknowledgment, and the acknowledgment icon (in the ACK. STATUS column) will be visible in the monitor until the acknowledgment arrives.

4. If you don't want to wait for acknowledgments, you can turn this function off by executing report IDX_NOALE (see Figure 5.18) from Transaction SE38. You can turn off requests for acknowledgments either for an entire application system or for a particular message type only.

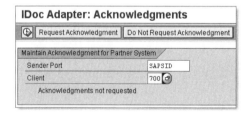

Figure 5.18 An IDoc Adapter's Acknowledgment Configuration

The correct configuration of requests for acknowledgments lets you better monitor IDocs because you will not see waiting statuses if you do not want to see them.

5.3.4 ALE Acknowledgments as SAP NetWeaver PI Request Messages

In standard ALE, acknowledgment messages (ALEAUD) are passed to SAP NetWeaver PI as SAP NetWeaver PI acknowledgment messages only. This means that when they are received by the SAP NetWeaver PI Integration Engine, they will be linked to a standard SAP NetWeaver PI request message and will not be processed any further. Figure 5.19 shows how SAP NetWeaver PI handles an ALE acknowledgment message for which no IDoc was found. The message is stopped with an error—ALEAUDIT IDoc CANNOT FIND REQUEST IDoc IN INTEGRATION SERVER—as you can see in Figure 5.19.

```
<?xml version="1.0" encoding="UTF-8" standalone="yes" ?>
<!-- Inbound Message   -->
- <SAP:Error xmlns:SAP="http://sap.com/xi/XI/Message/30"
    xmlns:SOAP="http://schemas.xmlsoap.org/soap/envelope/"
    SOAP:mustUnderstand="1">
    <SAP:Category>XIAdapter</SAP:Category>
    <SAP:Code area="IDOC_ADAPTER">ATTRIBUTE_NO_REQUEST</SAP:Code>
    <SAP:P1 />
    <SAP:P2 />
    <SAP:P3 />
    <SAP:P4 />
    <SAP:AdditionalText />
    <SAP:ApplicationFaultMessage namespace="" />
    <SAP:Stack>ALEAUDIT IDoc cannot find request IDoc in Integration
      Server</SAP:Stack>
    <SAP:Retry>N</SAP:Retry>
  </SAP:Error>
```

Figure 5.19 ALEAUD Message Without a Request IDoc

The error here is supposed to show that in the standard, ALEAUD messages are not treated as normal SAP NetWeaver PI request messages but as a different type of message. But what if there is a need to send them to a different system directly? As of service pack 08 for SAP NetWeaver PI 7.0 (SP17 for XI 3.0), it is possible to receive ALEAUD messages as normal SAP NetWeaver PI request messages. As of the service packs mentioned, there is a new report IDX_ALEREQUEST. When you open this report in Transaction SE38, you will see a set of parameters you need to fill, as shown in Figure 5.20:

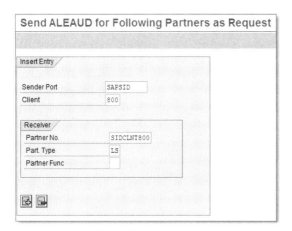

Figure 5.20 IDX_ALEREQUEST Report

▶ **Sender port**

The port of the SAP application system from which the ALEAUD will be received in SAP NetWeaver PI—these ports are maintained in Transaction IDX1.

▶ **Client**

The client of the SAP application system from which the ALEAUD will be received in SAP NetWeaver PI.

▶ **Receiver**

The receiver to which ALAUD message was sent—in most cases, this will be your SAP NetWeaver PI system.

▶ **Part. Type**

If you set up your PI system as a logical system in Transaction WE20 of the SAP application system the value for Partner Type will be LS (Logical system) in most cases.

▶ **Partner Func**

Optional you can specify a partner function of the receiver system—if it's used in partner profile configuration (Transaction WE20) of the SAP application system.

After you add the desired systems using the INSERT icon and confirm the entry by pressing F8 (EXECUTE button), the systems will be added to the acknowledgment exception table and will not be processed as acknowledgments any longer. When you now try to send an ALEAUD message from an SAP application system without any additional configuration (done in the Integration Directory), you should see an error message like the one shown in Figure 5.21: NO RECEIVER COULD BE DETERMINED.

```
<?xml version="1.0" encoding="UTF-8" standalone="yes" ?>
<!-- Receiver Identification   -->
- <SAP:Error xmlns:SAP="http://sap.com/xi/XI/Message/30"
    xmlns:SOAP="http://schemas.xmlsoap.org/soap/envelope/"
    SOAP:mustUnderstand="">
    <SAP:Category>XIServer</SAP:Category>
    <SAP:Code
      area="RCVR_DETERMINATION">NO_RECEIVER_CASE_ASYNC</SAP:Code>
    <SAP:P1 />
    <SAP:P2 />
    <SAP:P3 />
    <SAP:P4 />
    <SAP:AdditionalText />
    <SAP:ApplicationFaultMessage namespace="" />
    <SAP:Stack>No receiver could be determined</SAP:Stack>
    <SAP:Retry>M</SAP:Retry>
  </SAP:Error>
```

Figure 5.21 ALEAUD Message as an SAP NetWeaver PI Request Message

This means that from now on, ALEAUD messages from the configured SAP application system are treated as normal SAP NetWeaver PI request messages and you need to configure the SAP NetWeaver PI flow (especially the Integration Directory part) for SAP NetWeaver PI to know to which system ALEAUD IDocs need to be delivered.

This section provided you with all of the information required to be able to send IDocs from the SAP application system to SAP NetWeaver PI. The next section will show you how to configure the sending of IDocs in the other direction, from SAP NetWeaver PI to the SAP application system.

5.4   Sending IDocs from SAP NetWeaver PI

To start sending IDocs from SAP NetWeaver PI to an SAP application system, you have to configure both ends of the transmission (as you did when sending IDocs to SAP NetWeaver PI). In the following description, we assume that the configuration on the SAP application system side is already done because it was described in the previous sections. We also assume that the configuration is exactly the same as shown in this book.

In this section, you will create a sample scenario that will send a test IDoc to the SAP application system. To be more precise, you will send an IDOC-XML from a Web page to SAP NetWeaver PI, and the IDoc will be routed to one of your SAP application systems.

There are two things to be done for the ABAP portion (ABAP stack via SAP GUI) of SAP NetWeaver PI. First, you need an RFC destination to the SAP application system. You can use the one whose configuration was shown in the previous section (Transaction IDX1). Second, you need to load IDoc metadata with Transaction IDX2.

Integration Repository

You can start with the configuration on the Integration Repository side. Open it by clicking the Integration Repository link on the main Integration Builder page, Transaction SXMB_IFR in the SAP GUI. Proceed as follows:

1. First, you need to import a software component from the SLD using the following menu path in the repository: TOOLS • TRANSFER FROM THE SYSTEM LANDSCAPE DIRECTORY • IMPORT SOFTWARE COMPONENT VERSION.

2. You can either select a standard software component version (which is what we will do in our example) or use your own if you created it inside the SLD. Figure 5.22 shows how you can import a software component version created in the SLD in the Integration Repository. Select the checkbox on the standard software component and confirm the transfer.

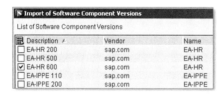

Figure 5.22 Import of Software Component Versions

3. After you import the software component version, you need to open it by double-clicking it and performing additional configuration (see Figure 5.23).

   ▷ First, you need to enable the software component version to import the RFC and IDocs signatures. To accomplish this, select IMPORT OF RFC AND IDOC INTERFACES FROM SAP SYSTEMS PERMITTED.

▷ Fill in CONNECTION DATA FOR IMPORT FROM SAP SYSTEM: For SYSTEM. Here, you have to fill in the SAP SID of your SAP application system. For CLIENT, select the client number of your SAP application system. These values can be taken from the SAP LOGON PROPERTIES tab.

▷ Create a new namespace for your scenario, for example `http://yourcompany.com/name_of_the_interface`. You can select any other namespace, depending on the naming conventions you need to use.

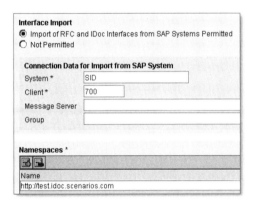

Figure 5.23 Importing an IDocs' Signatures

4. Saving the configuration will cause a new object menu—IMPORTED OBJECTS—appear at the bottom of your software component. To use IDocs in all scenarios in SAP NetWeaver PI, you not only need to have their metadata (to transform an IDoc to its XML form) in the ABAP portion but also their signatures (which are used during the design phase for mappings, etc.) from the SAP application system. You can easily download these from any application system by right-clicking the new IMPORTED OBJECTS menu and selecting IMPORT OF SAP OBJECTS from the context menu.

5. After you fill in the mandatory data (application system, user, etc.), SAP NetWeaver PI will download all IDoc names from the target SAP application system, as shown in Figure 5.24.

6. Activating the checkbox to select the IDoc names you want to use in this scenario and clicking CONTINUE will make their signatures appear in the software component version. In our test scenario, we do not want to use any kind of mapping, so you do not have to create any other objects such as message mappings or interface mappings.

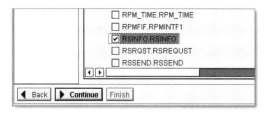

Figure 5.24 An IDoc's Signature Import

Note

When using IDocs, you do not have to create message type objects or message interfaces unless you want to use your IDocs in a business process. Only in such cases do you need to create an abstract message interface for the IDoc messages.

7. To finish the configuration on the Integration Repository side, from the main menu, you need to activate all changes on the CHANGE LIST tab (see Figure 5.25).

Figure 5.25 Change List Tab—Object Activation

The objects activated will be IDoc signature, software component, and so on.

Integration Directory

The second part of the configuration involves using the Integration Directory. Here, you will specify all of the routing conditions for the IDoc message flow. You have already imported the SAP application system into the Integration Directory; that is why you now only need to create an additional service that will correspond to the HTTP sender system. Therefore, you will create a business service, which represents an abstract unit of senders and receivers of messages.

1. To create a business service, you have to access the OBJECTS tab of the Integration Directory, select SERVICE WITHOUT PARTY, right-click BUSINESS SERVICE, and enter a name for it, for example HTTP_TEST_SERVICE.

2. To be able to configure the scenario using the Integration Directory configuration wizard, you need to add the IDoc message as an outbound interface on the SENDER tab of the business service (see Figure 5.26).

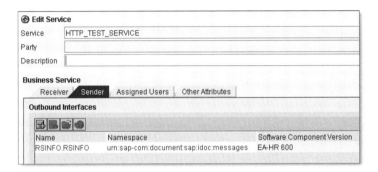

Figure 5.26 Business Service Sender Interfaces

Note

The term *outbound interface* means that the message will be sent to SAP NetWeaver PI because it is outbound from the sender system's point of view. The same applies to *inbound interfaces*, which are used to send messages from SAP NetWeaver PI to the destination system.

---

3. You can then press [F4] on the name of the interface and select the appropriate IDoc message.

4. For the next steps, a configuration wizard will help you with the creation of all objects necessary to perform simple scenarios. After you select the configuration wizard from the Integration Directory menu, select INTERNAL COMMUNICATION (see Figure 5.27) because you will be testing the scenario within your system landscape. This means there will be no involvement by external parties, which sometimes requires additional changes in the message header.

Figure 5.27 Configuration Wizard

5. On the next screen (see Figure 5.28), you have to select information about the sender, as follows:

▷ **Service Type**
Business service, because you want to send a message from your business service.

▷ **Service**
The business service created in the previous step, here HTTP_TEST_SERVICE.

▷ **Interface**
This holds the IDoc message (here RSINFO.RSINFO).

▷ **Namespace**
This should be filled automatically from the interface added in the previous step.

▷ **Adapter Type**
Because you will be testing the IDoc with a test tool, select the HTTP adapter.

Figure 5.28 Integration Directory Configuration Wizard

6. In the next screen, you only have to fill in the channel's name. You can use the standard convention presented by the SAP system (`<type>_<direction>_<opt. object>`). Here, `<type>` is the adapter metadata name (HTTP, IDoc, etc.), `<direction>` means the value in or out, and in some cases, you can use an additional object with the `<opt. object>` placeholder (such as `localAdapterEngine`).

Finally, you can add all of the new objects to one configuration scenario that will be created when you fill its name in the CONFIGURATION SCENARIO field. Configuration scenarios serve mainly to group directory objects. Proceed as follows:

1. Again, you can use the standard convention presented by the SAP system: `<scenario ID>_<self-explanatory name>`, where `<scenario ID>` is a unique identifier for configuration scenarios and `<self-explanatory name>` stands for a descriptive name, using upper case.

> **Note**
>
> When there are hundreds of directory objects, it is difficult to find them without configuration scenarios. For this reason, try to group them during the creation of the very first objects in the Integration Directory.

2. Before you can activate the objects, you have to finish the communication channel configuration (IDOC RECEIVER channel only), as shown in Figure 5.29.

   ▷ **RFC Destination**
   Points to the RFC destination to the SAP application system; this can be the same RFC destination you used in Transaction IDX1.

   ▷ **Interface Version**
   Select the appropriate version for your SAP application system release.

   ▷ **Port**
   Specifies the port used in Transaction IDX1.

   ▷ **SAP Release**
   Select the appropriate name of your SAP application system release (such as `470`, `640`, etc.).

   ▷ **Apply Control Record Values from Payload**
   Uncheck this option because we want to use the default values of the control record, filled in by SAP NetWeaver PI at runtime.

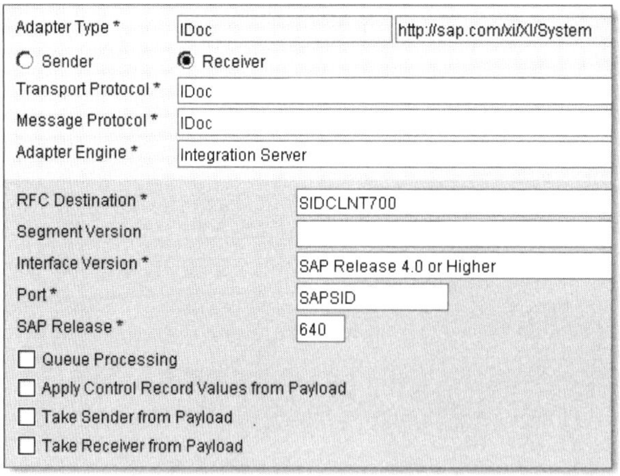

Figure 5.29 IDoc Adapter Configuration

In our sample scenario, we want SAP NetWeaver PI to fill the IDoc control record with default values, but you can influence these values by adjusting specific objects. The most important of these is the SENDER SYSTEM field filled in at runtime. If you do not configure any additional settings and try to test the scenario, SAP NetWeaver PI will not be able to convert the business service HTTP_TEST_SERVICE for an ALE logical system.

You can enter a logical system name in the business service object, but you have to take into consideration that these names are unique. As a result, SAP NetWeaver PI will not let you use the same name again.

However, there is an option that allows reuse of a logical system name in all IDoc scenarios. This is called a *header mapping*. You can select it when you open a receiver agreement created for your scenario. Figure 5.30 shows the header mapping filled in.

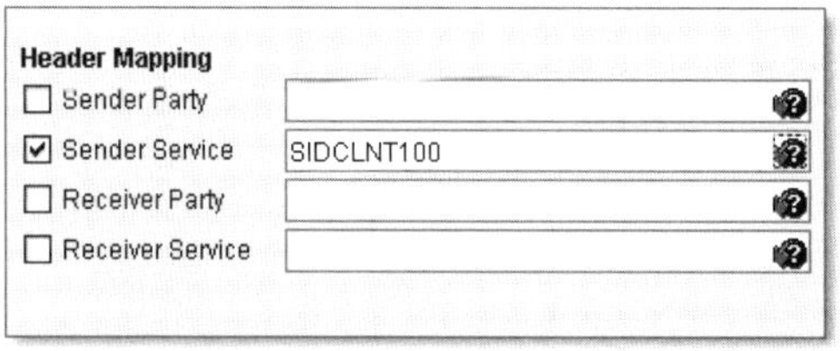

Figure 5.30 Header Mapping

With this option, you can tell SAP NetWeaver PI to use the logical system name of any previously configured system. If you perform the partner profile configuration in the SAP application system for only one external system (e.g., the Integration Server), you can specify that in your scenario, the logical system used for sending IDocs will be the one used by the sender service for your Integration Server.

Testing Sending IDocs

For testing this scenario, you will use the Runtime Workbench test tool to send an IDOC-XML message to SAP NetWeaver PI, and then the IDoc will be sent to the SAP application system. Proceed as follows:

1. First, you have to log in to the Runtime Workbench (Transaction SXMB_IFR).
2. Next, you have to select COMPONENT MONITORING • INTEGRATION ENGINE.
3. Then, select the TEST MESSAGE tab. You are ready to send a test IDoc message directly to the Integration Server.
4. Now, you have to fill in a few values, all of which can be found in the SENDER AGREEMENT in your business scenario in the Integration Directory (see Figure 5.31).

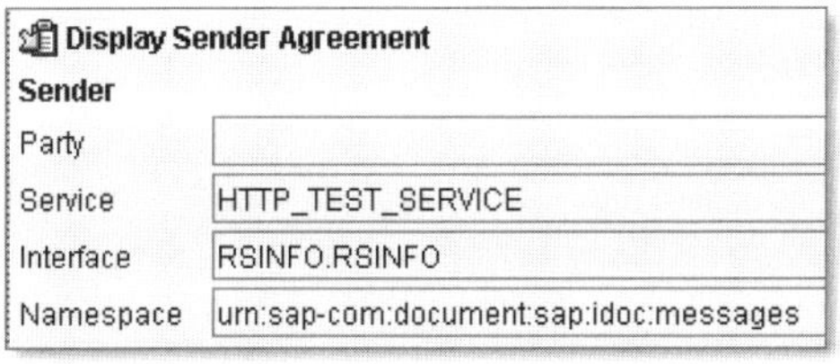

Figure 5.31 Sender Agreement

5. After you fill in the user and password in the USER and PASSWORD fields, paste an IDOC-XML message from Listing 5.2 into the PAYLOAD field. The IDOC-XML from Listing 5.2 is just an example; you can change the values if you wish.

```
<?xml version="1.0" encoding="UTF-8"?>
<RSINFO>
    <IDOC BEGIN="">
        <E1RSHIN SEGMENT="">
            <REQUEST>test value</REQUEST>
```

```
        <INFOIDOCNR>test</INFOIDOCNR>
        <SELDATE>test</SELDATE>
        <SELTIME/>
        <RQSTATE/>
        <RQRECORD/>
      </E1RSHIN>
    </IDOC>
  </RSINFO>
```

Listing 5.2 XML Test Message

6. You can try sending the test message by clicking the SEND button. If you carried out all of the configuration properly, you should see a success message (checkered flag) in the message monitor (Transaction SXMB_MONI) in SAP NetWeaver PI (see Figure 5.32).

Figure 5.32 Message Monitoring in the Integration Server

7. The status of the IDoc in Figure 5.33 shows the IDoc data from Transaction WE02 on the SAP application system. Remember that this will not be successful unless you fill it with correct values; however, because this is a simple flow test, you will finish at this stage.

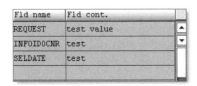

Figure 5.33 WE02—IDoc Message Monitoring in the SAP Application System

You should now be able to create basic IDoc flows through SAP NetWeaver PI in both directions: IDocs coming from the SAP application system to SAP NetWeaver PI and vice versa. In the next section, we will introduce more advanced topics and examples of how to monitor IDoc flows inside SAP NetWeaver PI.

5.5 Monitoring IDocs Inside SAP NetWeaver PI

There are two ways to monitor IDoc messages inside SAP NetWeaver PI. You can treat them as normal messages and monitor them with the XML message monitor using Transaction SXMB_MONI or SXI_MONITOR. Or, you can monitor your IDocs with Transaction IDX5, specifically designed for IDoc monitoring (see Figure 5.34).

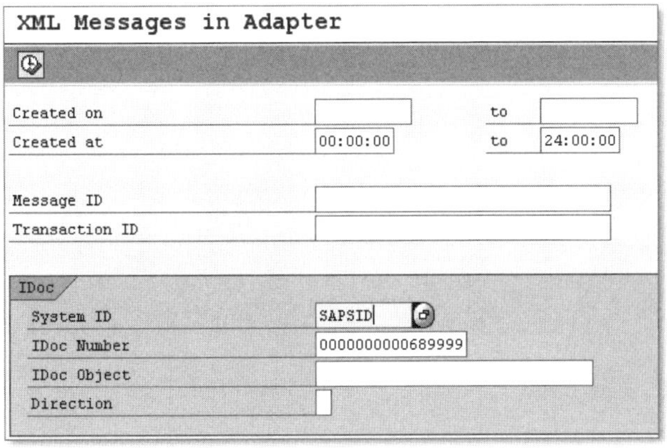

```
XML Messages in Adapter
 ⊕

Created on            [          ]   to  [          ]
Created at            [00:00:00]     to  [24:00:00]

Message ID            [                    ]
Transaction ID        [                    ]

 IDoc
   System ID          [SAPSID]  ⊕
   IDoc Number        [0000000000689999]
   IDoc Object        [                    ]
   Direction          [ ]
```

Figure 5.34 IDoc Message Monitoring Transaction

With Transaction IDX5, you do not have to specify the interface name, services, and so on. Instead, you can enter a system ID number to monitor all IDoc messages from one system or even enter an IDoc number from the source system and search by this criterion.

This is also the transaction from which you can easily go to the IDoc package monitor, which will be discussed in later sections. By double-clicking the IDoc message, you can proceed to the XML message monitor to see the message payload.

5.6 IDoc Control Record

EDI_DC40 is a well-known IDoc segment for any IDoc developer. It is called *IDoc control record* and contains information about the sender, receiver, IDoc number, message type, and so on. Many real-life scenarios are not IDoc-to-IDoc exchanges.

Instead, you may often have to post something coming to SAP NetWeaver PI in a format entirely different from that of an IDoc.

The IDoc receiver adapter provides you with several ways to work with the IDoc control record. Not only can you fill it using default values provided by the IDoc adapter during runtime, you can also fill in the values yourself in the mapping. First, we will look at using default values. Follow these steps:

1. If you do not want to fill the IDoc control record and instead use the default IDoc receiver adapter values, you can disable segment EDI_DC40 in the target IDoc in the Integration Repository. To do so, right-click the EDI_DC40 segment and select DISABLE from the context menu in the message mapping (see Figure 5.35).

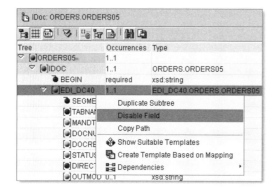

Figure 5.35 Disabling Fields in the Message Mapping

2. You also have to deactivate the APPLY CONTROL RECORD VALUES FROM PAYLOAD indicator in the IDoc Receiver channel in the Integration Directory (see Figure 5.36).

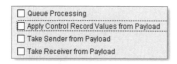

Figure 5.36 IDoc Adapter Configuration Parameters

3. If you finish the first two steps, the default values filled by SAP NetWeaver PI during the flow will be exactly as outlined in Table 5.1.

Field name	Value
SNDPOR	Constant SAP+SID (system ID) of the Integration Server
MANDT	Client number of the Integration Server
RCVPOR	Determined from the port in the receiver IDoc adapter.
ARCKEY	Message GUID
SERIAL	Determined from the control record of the IDoc XML payload.
MESTYP	Value taken from the SAP NetWeaver PI interfaces (You specify the MESTYP during the import of the IDoc's signature into the Integration Repository.)
IDOCTYP	Value taken from the SAP NetWeaver PI interfaces (You specify the IDOCTYP during the import of the IDoc's signature into the Integration Repository.)
CIMTYP	Value taken from the SAP NetWeaver PI interfaces (You specify the CIMTYP during the import of the IDoc's signature into the Integration Repository.)
SNDPRN	From SAP NetWeaver PI sender service
SNDPRT	Constant = LS
RCVPRN	From SAP NetWeaver PI receiver service
RCVPRT	Constant = LS
CREDAT	Date created
CRETIM	Time created

Table 5.1 An IDoc's Control Record Fields Descriptions

Changing the IDoc Control Record's Default Values

However, in most situations you need to control the IDoc control record values, and SAP NetWeaver PI provides you with two ways of doing so.

If the source system sends information that can be used to fill the IDoc control values during the mapping, you can easily use them inside this mapping. That is, you can map the appropriate values from the control record of the sender system to the control record of the receiver system.

Selecting the Apply Control Record Values from Payload indicator is not enough to set sender and receiver partners. If you use only this indicator, the only values that will be allowed to change during the mapping are MESCOD, MESCFT, TEST, EXPRSS, STD, STDVRS, STDMES, SNDSAD, SNDLAD, RCVSAD, RCVLAD, REFINT, REF-GRP. In our test case, however, we need to change the sender and receiver.

The Sender and Receiver fields can only be filled if you also select the Take Sender from Payload and Take Receiver from Payload indicators, as shown in Figure 5.37.

Figure 5.37 IDoc Adapter Configuration Parameters

There is another option, which is a combination of the two previously described options: You can change the sender and receiver without filling the IDoc control record in the mapping.

The header mapping option described earlier supports this approach, and is available when specifying the receiver agreement. You can select one of the already created business systems as a sender or receiver in the header mapping (see Figure 5.38), and the IDoc control record will be filled with the name of the logical system assigned to this business system during runtime.

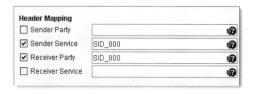

Figure 5.38 Header Mapping

The header mapping function also provides you with a more popular and simpler option of specifying a partner profile rather than a logical system. As shown in Table 5.1, the SNDPRT and RCVPRT fields will be filled with the LS value in the standard, which means that you can only process IDocs with the logical system partner profile set in your SAP application system. If you want to use any other partner profile, you can change this value by setting a different RECEIVER PARTY in the header mapping.

After you open the receiver party editor (see Figure 5.39), an "extended" option is available that allows you to select an XPATH expression for replacing the IDoc receiver. The IDoc receiver will be taken from the payload, and you can also set the schema as either an XPath expression or as a constant value. This will tell the IDoc receiver adapter to use this partner profile during the message flow.

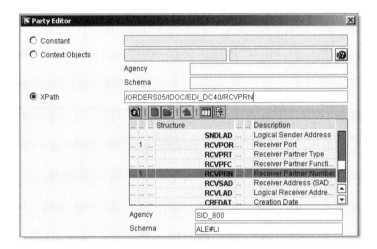

Figure 5.39 XPath Selection for IDoc Partner Changes

To summarize, IDoc monitoring and control record configuration are very common tasks, which you should be able to perform after reading the information in this section.

5.7 IDoc Packages and Event-Driven Messages

In many situations, you do not want your IDocs to be processed immediately after they come into SAP NetWeaver PI. The following are possible reasons:

▶ You need to send large volumes of master data IDocs, and you do not want to do this during normal business hours (during the day). Instead, you decide to send master data synchronization IDocs only at night.

▶ You create an integration process in SAP NetWeaver PI that collects multiple IDoc messages and sends them as a single bundle to certain third-party systems. These IDocs are being sent from an SAP R/3 or SAP ECC application system throughout the day. To not create instances of integration processes that will consume memory all day long, you can start them when a certain number of IDocs reach the SAP NetWeaver PI Integration Engine.

Note

The *integration process* in SAP NetWeaver PI is a cross-system process you can implement to define more complex message exchanges that can involve several steps. The processing of an integration process is also known as *Cross-Component Business Process Management* (CCBPM).

To be able to achieve the two scenarios described, SAP provides you with functionality called *IDoc packages* that are a part of *event-driven message processing*. With this functionality, you can schedule IDoc processing inside the Integration Engine. IDoc packages allow you to specify how many IDocs from one interface need to reach SAP NetWeaver PI to start processing inside the Integration Engine.

5.7.1 Setting Up IDoc Packages

The first thing you need to set up IDoc packages is to have a message ID. Follow these steps:

1. You can get a message ID from Transaction SXMB_MONI (see Figure 5.40), when opening one of the XML messages.

Status	Executed Until	Sender Interface	Message ID
	22.04.2006	MATMAS.MATMAS05	E0E46F09E8C09942A80BC7D076294536
	22.04.2006	MATMAS.MATMAS05	05E07465399AED4C9D2EE6A8FDFAAA22
	22.04.2006	MATMAS.MATMAS05	985A5FD75BAF9343B21CA945889911F8
	22.04.2006	MATMAS.MATMAS05	9E5E5BAF2D96184FB1E1B0C204686B2E

Figure 5.40 Message Monitoring Transaction

2. You can also get a message ID directly from the IDoc package's activation transaction (IDXPW), by using the input help on the MESSAGE ID field.

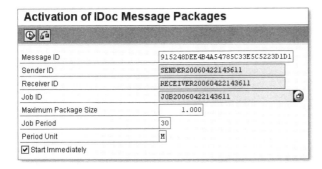

Figure 5.41 IDoc Package Activation

3. When you specify the MESSAGE ID, the SENDER ID, RECEIVER ID, and JOB ID will be filled automatically (see Figure 5.41). The MAXIMUM PACKAGE SIZE is the most important field. It defines the number of IDocs the job will wait for before it starts processing the IDocs as normal flows in the Integration Engine.

Setting a value of 50 means that only when 50 IDocs have reached SAP NetWeaver PI are the IDocs processed. Until then, they are visible in Transaction IDXP (monitor for message packages) with a waiting status, as shown in Figure 5.42.

When the number of IDocs specified during the package activation is reached, the IDocs are released for processing.

StatusGrpg	Message ID	Job ID
	DDE3C0E50F7A8C419B5B62F	JOB20060422143611
	00B2C72BEC16314BB396414	JOB20060422143611
	AD1D4FC5A1D4B5419CDF40!	JOB20060422143611
	F7771440A4F7E743B0FCDC0	JOB20060422143611
	2402198240C5524CB706F33f	JOB20060422143611

Messages for Package 5

Figure 5.42 Message Package

4. If the requirements change and you need to process the messages sooner, there are at least two ways of doing so. You can process messages individually from Transaction IDXP, monitor for message packages, by selecting a message and clicking the appropriate button (UNPACK) or pressing ⬆+F6. The second option can be used for more automatic message processing. If you always want to process all remaining messages at a certain time, you can schedule report

SXMS_UNPACK_MESSAGES, shown in Figure 5.43, which allows you to unpack all of the packages. All you need to do to start the report is fill the TIME field and execute.

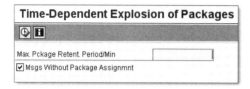

Figure 5.43 Unpacking Transaction for Integration Server Messages

5.7.2 Advanced Scheduling of Message Processing

However, setting the maximum package size during the activation of IDoc packages is not the only option for starting IDoc processing. The event-driven message processing scheduler allows more complex, time-dependent scheduling of IDoc messages. The time-dependent unpacking of packages function cannot be used to schedule unpacking of a single message type because it unpacks all message types at once. If you use the standard scheduler, however, you can schedule processing of individual messages. Proceed as follows:

1. The starting point is the same as with IDoc Packages: Transaction IDXPW.

2. Next, you need to modify the automatically created START MESSAGES IMMEDI-ATELY indicator, which tells the Integration Engine to start processing messages as soon as the condition (MAXIMUM PACKAGE SIZE) is met (see Figure 5.44).

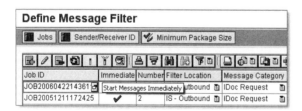

Figure 5.44 Message Filter Definition

3. You can change the START MESSAGES IMMEDIATELY indicator to EVENT-DRIVEN MESSAGE PACKAGE PROCESSING. To do so, double-click the START MESSAGES IM-MEDIATELY indicator, and select the new processing type.

4. To change the indicator, you have to deactivate the message filter, change the setting, save it, and activate it again. After the indicator has been changed, you can use the Jobs menu to schedule the messages (see Figure 5.45). Here, you can specify the Period and Period Unit (minutes, hours, and days).

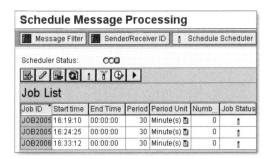

Figure 5.45 Message Scheduler

5. When the specific start time is met, the messages will be processed exactly as they were when the maximum package size was reached after the Start Message Package Immediately indicator was set to run automatically.

Note

The scheduler will work only if the scheduler's status is green. To start the scheduler, you need to activate it first. This can be done from the schedule message processing transaction, Transaction SXMSJOBS, by clicking the Schedule Scheduler button.

5.8 Sender IDoc Adapter Packaging – Enhancement Package 1 for SAP NetWeaver PI 7.0

One of the typical requirements when sending IDocs to external systems is having the ability to send multiple IDocs as one message. All SAP application systems capable of using IDocs as message interfaces (SAP ERP, SCM, CRM, etc.) have always had the option to collect IDocs in the outbound partner profile. Thus, you have always been able to specify the following:

▶ **Pack. Size**
The package size determines the number of IDocs sent from the SAP application system in one RFC call—the greater the package size, the more IDocs will be delivered to an external system in one call.

▶ **Collect IDocs**
One of the options from the OUTPUT MODE options specifies that IDocs are not sent to the receiver system as soon as they are created but are instead collected and sent only when a special program, RSEOUT00, is executed.

Both of the options described are shown in Figure 5.46.

Figure 5.46 Outbound Partner Profile for IDoc Packaging

The problem with SAP NetWeaver PI 7.0 was that even if program RSEOUT00 was executed on the SAP application system, and as many IDocs as specified in the outbound partner profile were delivered to SAP NetWeaver PI, inside SAP NetWeaver PI, they were split into one IDoc for one SAP NetWeaver PI message principal. This is why it was impossible to receive multiple IDocs even if they were sent as described from the SAP application system. The only way to collect them again inside the Integration Engine of SAP NetWeaver PI was by using an integration process. Inside an integration process, you can collect different types of messages. The main problem with this approach is that it is an ineffective process that consumes a lot of system resources and memory.

SAP also noticed this and provided a new solution in SAP enhancement package 1 (EhP1) for SAP NetWeaver PI 7.0. With this new functionality, you can use IDoc packages created in an outbound partner profile inside SAP NetWeaver PI 7.0, with very little configuration effort. Four steps are involved, as follows:

1. You need to create a standard outbound partner profile inside the SAP application system and specify the package size and collect IDocs options exactly as shown in Figure 5.46 and as described in the text.

2. You need to change the IDoc occurrence as shown in Section 5.12 and create an external definition from this IDoc. This will allow you to have many IDocs in a single SAP NetWeaver PI message.

3. Next, you need to create a mapping inside which you will use the new IDoc's external definition as a source message, remembering that the mapping will now have many IDocs in the input (not just one, as was the case with the classic approach without EhP1).

4. You then need to specify two additional parameters inside of your IDoc sender adapter communication channel responsible for receiving IDocs from the SAP application system, as shown in Figure 5.47:

   ▶ IDOC-PACKAGING
     This checkbox enables IDoc packages on SAP NetWeaver PI for this particular communication channel.

   ▶ IDOC-PACKAGE SIZE
     This parameter specifies the maximum number of IDocs that can be placed into one IDoc XML message (SAP NetWeaver PI message).

Figure 5.47 Sender IDoc Adapter Packages—EhP1 Feature

After this configuration is completed, you can try sending a package of IDoc messages. If you generate a few IDocs inside your SAP application system, they will be collected as per the configuration. Executing report RSEOUT00 will release the entire package and send them to SAP NetWeaver PI, where you can monitor them using Transaction SXI_MONITOR, for example.

When you open an SAP NetWeaver PI message, you should see that it contains several IDocs (as many as specified in the outbound partner profile and sender IDoc adapter communication channel), as shown in Figure 5.48.

```
<?xml version="1.0" encoding="UTF-8" ?>
- <MBGMCR02>
  + <IDOC BEGIN="">
  + <IDOC BEGIN="">
  + <IDOC BEGIN="">
  + <IDOC BEGIN="">
  + <IDOC BEGIN="">
  + <IDOC BEGIN="">
  + <IDOC BEGIN="">
  + <IDOC BEGIN="">
  + <IDOC BEGIN="">
  + <IDOC BEGIN="">
  </MBGMCR02>
```

Figure 5.48 IDoc Package in the SAP NetWeaver PI Message Monitor

When using this new functionality, you need to keep three things in mind:

▶ An ALE audit IDoc message (ALEAUD) is created for each package, not for all IDocs inside the package.

▶ ALE audit messages from the SAP application system cannot be combined into packages.

If you specify IDoc packages' use inside the sender IDoc adapter communication channel, you cannot use IDoc tunnelling any longer (described in Section 5.8).The new IDoc packaging feature from EhP1 gives you not only faster processing time of IDocs inside the Integration Engine (because many SAP NetWeaver PI pipeline steps such as mappings, routings, and so on will only be executed once per package and not once per each IDoc), it also allows you to not use integration processes to collect IDocs when the receiver application requires this. For these reasons, you will probably want to use this functionality in quite a few cases.

5.9   IDoc Tunneling

In most cases, the development of IDoc flows will require some structure or value changes involving lookup tables, conversions, and so on. However, there might be a situation when you need neither structure nor value conversion. This can happen with a very simple flow, such as transferring IDocs between systems with no message changes. Or, it can happen when the flow was designed and created before the use of a middleware platform.

5.9.1 Sending IDocs Without XML Conversion

Every message that reaches the SAP NetWeaver PI Integration Engine is converted to an XML message that is part of the SOAP payload (see Figure 5.49).

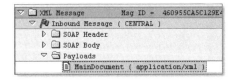

Figure 5.49 XML Payload, Message Monitor

There are a few cases, however, in which SAP NetWeaver PI does not have to convert messages to their XML representation. By no means are IDocs XML structures when they are sent from SAP application systems. As a result, if you do not use any mappings, you can set configuration parameters to not convert every IDoc into an XML message but rather to push them through in the form of IDoc tables. This is essentially the same format in which they are received by SAP NetWeaver PI. You can use this functionality in the following situations:

▸ When migrating the mentioned IDoc flows into SAP NetWeaver PI because you want to monitor all flows from one application monitoring transaction of SAP NetWeaver PI or Runtime Workbench.

▸ When sending IDoc data that does not require any conversions.

The next sections provide you with detailed descriptions of the configuration settings for IDoc tunneling.

5.9.2 Setting Up IDoc Tunneling

To enable IDoc tunneling, the XML_CONVERSION parameter has to be changed. XML_CONVERSION is one of the Integration Engine's parameters used for specifying how the engine should work with IDOC-XML messages. Proceed as follows:

1. Enter Transaction SXMB_ADM (Integration Engine configuration) and select EDIT • CHANGE SPECIFIC CONFIGURATION DATA. The XML_CONVERSION parameter belongs to the IDoc category parameters and can have three different values, as described in Table 4.2.

2. In our example, we want every IDoc to be saved as a table, without any XML conversion. Therefore, set the current value to 0 (see Figure 5.50).

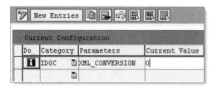

Figure 5.50 Integration Engine Configuration

Value	Description
0	Every IDoc is saved as a table, and there is no IDOC-XML conversion inside the Integration Engine.
1	Every IDoc is converted to IDOC-XML, whether or not the service needs it.
2	An IDoc is converted to IDOC-XML only when this kind of process is requested by the calling service.

Table 5.2 Possible Values of the XML_CONVERSION Parameter

3. When you test any IDoc flow without a mapping program, you will see that the IDoc was not converted to an XML message (does not have the type `application/xml`). Instead, it is saved as an IDoc table with type `application/x-sap.idoc.bin`, as specified in the configuration parameter (see Figure 5.51).

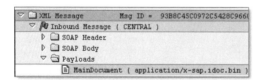

Figure 5.51 Message Monitoring Transaction—IDoc Not in XML Format

Setting XML_CONVERSION correctly can significantly speed up many IDoc flows, and in some cases it can even improve the overall performance of SAP NetWeaver PI. This is because it relieves the Integration Engine of the need to perform memory-consuming parsing of the IDoc messages, which in many cases is not necessary at all. If you send IDocs from one SAP application system to another without any mappings, it is highly advisable to use IDoc tunneling whenever possible.

5.10   IDoc Acknowledgments

When using synchronous communication, you wait for the answer from the target system to send the response to the source system. You always know the status of the application on the other end, because there can be only the following few statuses:

▶ The message broker (such as SAP NetWeaver PI) cannot get to the target system. As a result, it sends an error message to the source system.

▶ The message reached the target system but there is no response; the message broker can send an error message to the source system.

▶ The message reached the target system and the target system responded; the response can be passed to the source system.

In all of the above cases, you know exactly what is happening with the flow at all times: whether it is waiting, reached the timeout, or was successful. But what if you use asynchronous flows?

IDocs are a typical example of asynchronous communication in which SAP NetWeaver PI does not wait for a response. However, there is a way to monitor these flows using *acknowledgments*. Acknowledgments are messages sent from SAP NetWeaver PI to the SAP application system or the other way round that provide information on the status of the original message.

There are two main types of acknowledgments used in IDoc scenarios using SAP NetWeaver PI. They are as follows:

▶ **System acknowledgment**
This acknowledgment is sent when the message reaches the target system.

▶ **Application acknowledgment**
This acknowledgment is sent when the target application processes the inbound message.

Both of these acknowledgment types can have either a positive or a negative status. The status is positive when the message reaches the target system or is correctly processed by the receiving application. The status is negative when the message does not reach the target or the application could not process the message. SAP NetWeaver PI supports both types of acknowledgments; they will be described in the next sections.

183

5.10.1 Sending Acknowledgments from an SAP Application System

IDoc acknowledgments from the SAP application system, which are also called *ALE audit messages*, are very well known to anyone who has ever worked with IDocs. SAP R/3 and ECC systems allow you to generate acknowledgments that describe the processing status of the original IDocs. On the other hand, SAP NetWeaver PI can work with these acknowledgments natively, without any specific configuration.

1. To receive acknowledgment messages from the different SAP systems in SAP NetWeaver PI, you only need to set up the RECEIVER IDoc communication channel (see Figure 5.52) that will be used for sending IDocs to the SAP R/3 or SAP ECC system.

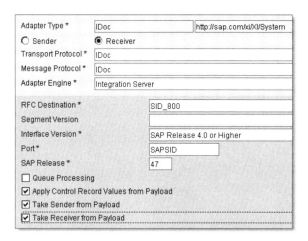

Figure 5.52 Receiver IDoc Adapter Configuration

No other configuration is required. You do not need to configure any routing. If there are many receiver IDoc communication channels pointing to one business system, the one whose name starts with "Ack" will be used to send acknowledgments.

2. The second part is the configuration of the SAP application system, to enable it to send acknowledgments. For this, you need to maintain a distribution model (Transaction BD64) created for your IDoc exchange in which you have to add the ALEAUD message type, as shown in Figure 5.53.

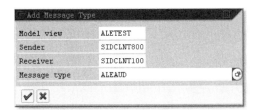

Figure 5.53 Adding Audit Message Configuration to the Distribution Model

3. If the distribution model is correct, you can maintain the outbound profile for the partner profile, which you use to receive IDocs from SAP NetWeaver PI. You need to use the following values in the partner profile configuration (Transaction WE20):

   ▸ MESSAGE TYPE: ALEAUD

   ▸ BASIC TYPE: ALEAUD01

4. After the distribution model and the partner profile are set up correctly, you can start generating acknowledgments for incoming IDocs. You can do this by running report RBDSTATE. In this report, you need to specify logical systems to which you want to send confirmations, IDoc message types and—most important—the time interval of the date when the IDocs were changed. In Figure 5.54, you can see the report and the fields you need to fill before executing it.

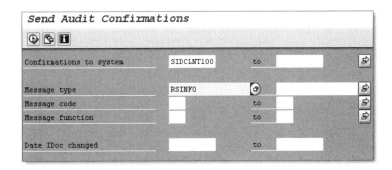

Figure 5.54 Report for Sending Audit Confirmations

5. When IDoc confirmations will be sent via RBDSTATE, the ACK. STATUS in the XML message monitor on the SAP NetWeaver PI side will show these confirmations as shown in Figure 5.55.

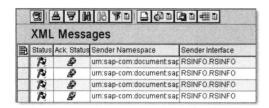

Figure 5.55 Message Monitoring Transaction — Acknowledgment Statuses

> **Note**
>
> Report RBDSTATE can be scheduled; thus, the confirmations may not be visible the very moment an IDoc reaches the SAP application system.

6. Next, the administrator can open the message and retrieve the acknowledgment information by selecting the correct confirmation message from Transaction SXI_MONITOR. He will see the error message generated on the SAP application system side (see Figure 5.56).

Figure 5.56 Message Monitoring Transaction — Acknowledgments

The status of the inbound IDoc can change; for example, when someone reprocesses the IDoc on the SAP application system. This is why many confirmation messages can be sent to the R/3 system for one IDoc. Remember that only the status of the last confirmation message is shown in the XML message monitor.

This section showed you how you can configure SAP NetWeaver PI to receive IDoc acknowledgments. In the next section, we will show you the configuration for sending acknowledgments.

5.10.2 Sending Acknowledgments from SAP NetWeaver PI

Aside from sending confirmation messages, the SAP application system can also receive them from other systems. SAP NetWeaver PI can be very easily configured for sending acknowledgements in many situations, including the following:

► When the target system cannot be reached.

► When there is a system error inside SAP NetWeaver PI.

To handle inbound ALE audits in the SAP application system, all you need to do is set the inbound profile for the partner that sends IDocs to SAP NetWeaver PI. You need to specify the following values:

► MESSAGE TYPE: ALEAUD

► PROCESS CODE: AUD1

SAP NetWeaver PI allows you to set up sending confirmation messages very easily. Follow these steps:

1. You only have to change one configuration parameter, `ACK_SYSTEM_FAILURE`, in the Integration Engine configuration (see Figure 5.57). Navigate there via SXMB_ADM • INTEGRATION ENGINE CONFIGURATION • EDIT • CHANGE SPECIFIC CONFIGURATION.

Figure 5.57 Integration Engine Configuration

When the `ACK_SYSTEM_FAILURE` parameter is set with the CURRENT VALUE 1, the Integration Engine will report system errors to all asynchronous messages that expect this kind of confirmation.

2. To analyze the information from the acknowledgment sent from SAP NetWeaver PI, you sometimes need to understand the message flow. Suppose that, in our integration scenarios, IDocs are being sent to a third-party system that communicates with SAP NetWeaver PI using any J2EE adapter. If the system is not available, you will not see the negative acknowledgment status of the outbound IDoc on the SAP R/3 or SAP ECC side when the very first negative acknowledgment arrives from SAP NetWeaver PI. In Figure 5.58, you can see

that the first negative acknowledgments did not change the IDoc's status to error. Instead, they only communicated that the IDocs are in the target system.

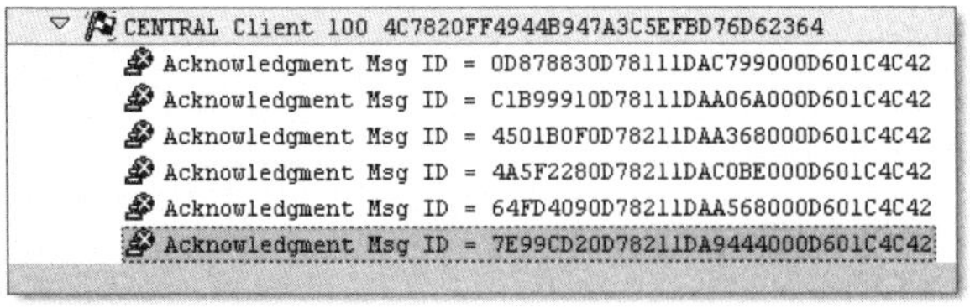

```
▽ CENTRAL Client 100 4C7820FF4944B947A3C5EFBD76D62364
   Acknowledgment Msg ID = 0D878830D78111DAC799000D601C4C42
   Acknowledgment Msg ID = C1B99910D78111DAA06A000D601C4C42
   Acknowledgment Msg ID = 4501B0F0D78211DAA368000D601C4C42
   Acknowledgment Msg ID = 4A5F2280D78211DAC0BE000D601C4C42
   Acknowledgment Msg ID = 64FD4090D78211DAA568000D601C4C42
   Acknowledgment Msg ID = 7E99CD20D78211DA9444000D601C4C42
```

Figure 5.58 Negative Acknowledgments from SAP NetWeaver PI's Point of View

Figure 5.59 shows an acknowledgment status from the SAP application system's perspective (Transaction WE02).

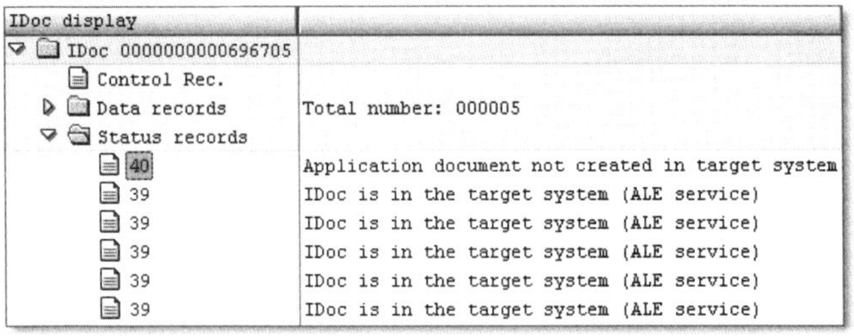

```
IDoc display
▽ IDoc 0000000000696705
   Control Rec.
 ▷ Data records        Total number: 000005
 ▽ Status records
     40                Application document not created in target system
     39                IDoc is in the target system (ALE service)
     39                IDoc is in the target system (ALE service)
     39                IDoc is in the target system (ALE service)
     39                IDoc is in the target system (ALE service)
```

Figure 5.59 Negative Acknowledgments from the SAP Application System's Point of View

3. The situation occurred because the Adapter Framework of SAP NetWeaver PI sent the negative acknowledgment every time it tried to reach the target system. Only when the last scheduled delivery has been executed and has not been successful does SAP NetWeaver PI send the PERMANENT ERROR acknowledgment message (see Listing 5.3). This changes the outbound IDoc status to 40, meaning that the IDoc did not reach the target system.

This kind of error can easily be found in the sender system, and the IDoc can be resent when the connection is working again.

```xml
<?xml version="1.0" encoding="UTF-8" standalone="yes" ?>
<!-- Response -->
<SAP:Ack xmlns:SAP="http://sap.com/xi/XI/Message/30"
  xmlns:SOAP="http://schemas.xmlsoap.org/soap/envelope/"
  SOAP:mustUnderstand="1">
    <SAP:Status>Error</SAP:Status>
```

```
        <SAP:Category>permanent</SAP:Category>
    </SAP:Ack>
```

Listing 5.3 Permanent Error in SOAP Message

IDoc acknowledgments from SAP NetWeaver PI can be used to identify IDocs with errors on sender systems, which can improve error identification and speed up resolution time. This is why it is good practice to frequently use acknowledgements.

5.11   IDoc Serialization

Some interface flows might have to be processed one by one and not in random order. For example, a material has to be created first before it can be sold; therefore, a message or an IDoc creating a material will have to be processed before a message or IDoc creating a sales order. In integration terms, we say we need to queue the message flows to be able to achieve real serialization.

SAP NetWeaver PI is not only a message transformation tool that allows changing of the messages' values or structures and sending of the data using different adapters, but it is also a tool for queuing messages. If a sender system cannot handle sending messages in order, SAP NetWeaver PI can start queuing the messages only when they reach one of the adapters.

The use of queues in IDoc scenarios has been dramatically improved with SAP Web Application Server (SAP Web AS) 6.40. The following scenarios are written as though the SAP application system uses at least Release 6.40.

Note

SAP NetWeaver Application Server (SAP NetWeaver AS) is a technological successor of the previous SAP Basis system and the SAP Web Application Server.

5.11.1   Setting Up Standard IDoc Serialization

If you want to queue IDoc flows, you need to first set up queue management in the SAP application system.

1. With an SAP application system based on SAP Web AS 6.40, you can do this during partner profile creation.

2. After you specify a transactional RFC port and select the QUEUE PROCESSING option, you can specify a RULE NAME that will generate the queue's name for your flow (see Figure 5.60). Rules can be maintained in Transaction WE85, and they can specify both constant or dynamic queue names.

3. The configuration shown in Figure 5.60 ensures that all IDocs sent using this outbound configuration will be placed in one queue, the name of which will contain two parts: SAP_ALE_ and the name generated by the rule.

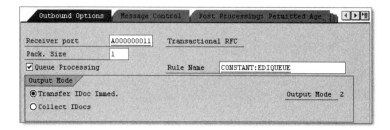

Figure 5.60 IDoc Configuration Transaction

4. After the IDoc is sent, you can see in the IDoc monitoring transactions (WE02 and WE05) that it has been processed via qRFC (see Figure 5.61).

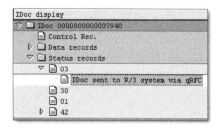

Figure 5.61 IDoc Monitoring Transaction

Note

Queued RFC (qRFC) is an enhanced tRFC that uses queues (inbound and outbound) to preserve the sequence of calls.

5. If the IDocs from the SAP application system cannot be sent to SAP NetWeaver PI, the calls can be monitored in Transaction SMQ1. In Figure 5.62, you can see that the function module IDOC_INBOUND_IN_QUEUE, which was used to send the

IDoc from the SAP application system, was called but was not successful. All of the IDocs are waiting in the same order they were created. You can see all error reasons in Transaction SMQ1 when you execute the transaction.

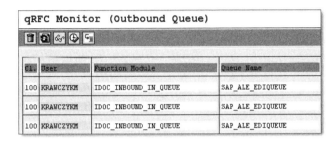

Figure 5.62 qRFC Monitor with IDoc Entries

6. To make sure that the order of calls will always be preserved, you can try executing any other call—generating a new IDoc, for example, via Transaction WE19—that is not the first one in the queue. You will receive a message that this cannot be done (see Figure 5.63) because other IDoc predecessors are waiting to be delivered first.

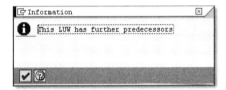

Figure 5.63 Logical Unit of Work

If you were to delete a *logical unit of work* (LUW) this might mean that the IDoc would never reach SAP NetWeaver PI. A LUW is an inseparable sequence of operations that can be either fully executed or not executed at all.

Therefore, it is highly inadvisable to delete LUWs on a production system. Instead, try to remove the error and restart the LUW later on.

Because the IDoc was delivered to the SAP NetWeaver PI IDoc adapter with the quality of service *exactly once in order* (EOIO), it can be processed in the same sequence (using the same queue) in which it was sent from the SAP application system.

> **Note**
>
> In SAP NetWeaver PI we distinguish three types of quality of service:
> ▶ **Best effort (BE)**
>   When a message is sent synchronously and waits for an answer.
> ▶ **Exactly once (EO)**
>   When a message is sent asynchronously.
> ▶ **Exactly once in order (EOIO)**
>   When a message is sent asynchronously with the name of the queue from the client application (or adapter), and the sequence of calls can be preserved within SAP NetWeaver PI.

The next example shows you how to configure SAP NetWeaver PI to maintain the sequence of calls during the outbound IDoc processing. Proceed as follows:

1. First, you need to specify the QUEUE PROCESSING option in the receiver IDoc adapter in the Integration Directory (see Figure 5.64).

Figure 5.64 Queue Processing Options in the IDoc Adapter

2. If the call to the receiving SAP application system is not successful, you will be able to monitor it the same way as you did in the SAP application system, using Transaction SMQ1. Because the IDoc in SAP NetWeaver PI is a standard SOAP message, however, you can see its structure by clicking the message TID in Transaction SMQ1.

3. To be able to see the IDoc from the queue monitor the same way as with Transaction IDX5, you need to register a display program: `IDX_SHOW_MESSAGE` (see Figure 5.65). You can do this in Transaction SMQE, navigate to EDIT • REGISTER DISPLAY PROGRAM, or press `Ctrl`+`F10`.

Figure 5.65 Registering the IDoc Display Program

4. When the program is registered for the corresponding queues, you can see IDoc messages directly from the queue monitor by double-clicking them.

If the flow does not work as expected, you may need to check the queue, and, in some cases, remove IDocs from the queue, as explained in the next section.

5.11.2   Removing IDocs from the Queues

If the system that is supposed to receive the IDoc is not based on SAP Web AS 6.40 or higher, the function module IDOC_INBOUND_IN_QUEUE cannot be used, and it will be automatically changed to IDOC_INBOUND_ASYNCHRONOUS. This is why setting the QUEUE PROCESSING indicator in the IDoc receiver channel does not make sense. Should you do so in this case, the IDoc messages would lose their EOIO quality of service—it will be changed to EO in the message header—and could be sent from SAP NetWeaver PI in random order.

1. To control individual queues, you can use two transactions: WEINBQUEUE and WEOUTQUEUE. They both allow you not only to monitor IDocs waiting in the queues but also to delete the queue entries that need to be removed.

2. You can delete the queue entry with the REMOVE IDOC FROM QUEUE button and then start the queue again. In Figure 5.66, you can see the IDoc queue administration transaction from which you can make the deletion.

Inbound IDoc Queue Display	Description
▽ ☐ IDoc Inbound Queue	
▽ ☐ SRPMNDT100	Sender
▽ ☐ SAP_ALE_EDIQUEUE	Queue
▷ 🗂 0000000000007767 | RSRQST	IDoc No. |Message Type
▽ 🗂 20IDocs from0000000000007768	IDocs in Interval
🗂 0000000000007768 | RSRQST	IDoc No. |Message Type
🗂 0000000000007769 | RSRQST	IDoc No. |Message Type
🗂 0000000000007770 | RSRQST	IDoc No. |Message Type
🗂 0000000000007771 | RSRQST	IDoc No. |Message Type
🗂 0000000000007772 | RSRQST	IDoc No. |Message Type

Figure 5.66 IDoc Queue Monitoring Transaction

5.11.3   Pseudo IDoc Serialization

The IDoc serialization we have described is only possible if your SAP application system is based on SAP Web Application Server 6.40 or SAP NetWeaver AS. But what if you use an older system?

There is an easy workaround that enables you to queue IDocs in the Integration Engine of SAP NetWeaver PI. You can specify a *queue ID* that will be used for all IDocs from the source SAP application system. To use this function, all you need to do is fill table IDXQUEUE in Transaction SE16 with the following appropriate values (see Figure 5.67):

▶ **PORT**
Here, you need to fill in the port of the SAP application system maintained in Transaction IDX1.

▶ **CLIENT**
Describes the client of the SAP application system.

▶ **MESTYP**
Specifies the message type of the IDoc.

▶ **QUEUEID**
This ID will be used later on by the Integration Engine to create a queue name.

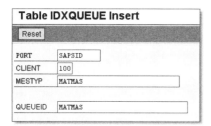

Figure 5.67 Maintenance of Table IDXQUEUE

With this functionality, IDocs will be processed inside SAP NetWeaver PI in the same sequence as they were received by the IDoc adapter. You do not have to maintain the sequence of the calls before the message got to the Integration Server and after it was sent by the IDoc receiver adapter.

This section described how to configure SAP NetWeaver PI in terms of queue-handling with IDoc scenarios. These are needed in many real-life projects because the flows need to run in a predefined order.

5.12   IDoc Bundling

Some interfaces require the use of multiple instances of the same IDoc. Suppose, for example, that you receive a file with dozens of material movements. What can you do with this file?

▶ You can either use a ccBPM and a message mapping within this ccBPM to create many material movement IDocs and send them one by one, or, you can make a small change in the IDoc structure to post all IDocs in one sending step. The problem with the ccBPM approach is that you will need to use the sending step in a loop to send one IDoc at a time. This will be rather time and resource intensive because the receiver IDoc adapter will have to try to log in to the SAP application server each time it receives an IDoc.

▶ If you do send all IDocs in one sending step, you will not only save resources but also dramatically reduce the execution time of your integration process. To be able to use multiple IDocs in one message, you need to change the IDoc's occurrence in your message.

The next section provides you with details on how to configure SAP NetWeaver PI to allow processing of multiple IDoc instances.

Multiple IDoc Instances in One Message

Changing the IDoc's occurrence in a message requires certain steps.

1. You first need to import the IDoc into the Integration Repository.

2. After the IDoc is imported, you need to export an IDoc into an XML schema definition (XSD) format. This can be done in the Tools • Export as XSD menu.

3. When you save the IDoc on your local disk, you need to open it (e.g., with the Notepad editor) and add the value `maxOccurs="unbounded"` after the IDoc's `type`, as shown in Figure 5.68.

4. The next step is to import the new definition as an external definition (in the Interface Objects menu) in the Integration Repository. To be able to select an XSD file, you need to change the external definition's category from *Web Services Description Language* (WSDL) to XSD.

5. After you upload the new definition, you can immediately use it in the mapping. Notice that the change in the IDoc's occurrence is reflected in the message mapping, as you can see in Figure 5.69.

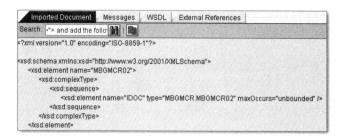

Figure 5.68 IDoc's XSD Schema with Changed Occurrence

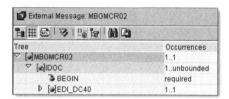

Figure 5.69 IDoc with Changed Occurrence

6. Now, the mapping can be used to create many IDocs. After the message mapping is finished, an interface mapping needs to be defined. One thing to remember here is that while specifying the target (if the target will be the enhanced IDoc definition), you should select the standard IDoc and not the external definition.

7. During the integration tests, you should be able to see (via Transaction SXI_MONITOR) that the IDoc structure can now contain many IDocs (see Figure 5.70). This can help make your interface much faster than it would be if you did not use this feature.

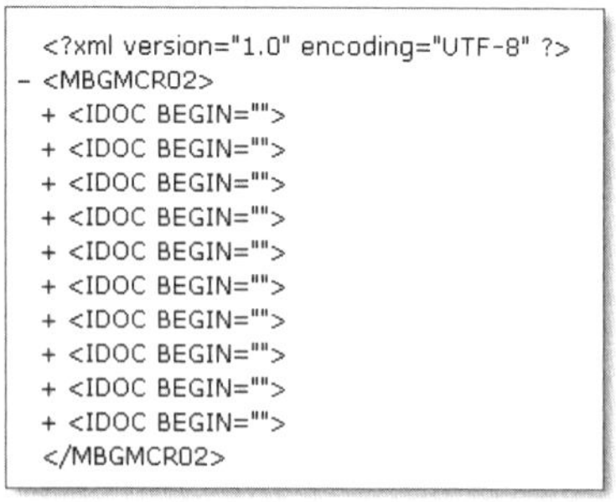

```
<?xml version="1.0" encoding="UTF-8" ?>
- <MBGMCR02>
  + <IDOC BEGIN="">
  + <IDOC BEGIN="">
  + <IDOC BEGIN="">
  + <IDOC BEGIN="">
  + <IDOC BEGIN="">
  + <IDOC BEGIN="">
  + <IDOC BEGIN="">
  + <IDOC BEGIN="">
  + <IDOC BEGIN="">
  + <IDOC BEGIN="">
  </MBGMCR02>
```

Figure 5.70 Many IDocs of the Same Type in One IDOC-XML

5.13   Turning Off IDoc Processing Within the Integration Engine

If there are any IDocs that you do not want to process using the Integration Engine, such as IDocs used for user management, you can place them into a special exception table. There, they will be handled by SAP NetWeaver PI as are the IDocs on the SAP application system.

1. You can place the IDoc into the exception table using report IDX_SELECT_ IDOCTYP_WITHOUT_IS (see Figure 5.71) from Transaction SE38, which takes only one parameter: the IDoc's basic type (IDOCTYP).

Figure 5.71 Removing IDocs from Processing by the Integration Engine

2. After the report has been executed and the IDoc's basic type has been inserted, you can check table IDXIDOCINB (with Transaction SE16) to see which IDocs are already included in this exception table.

> **Note**
>
> If you add the IDoc to the exception table, you need to perform standard IDoc configuration in your SAP NetWeaver PI system (via Transactions WE20, WE21, etc.) before you can process it.

5.14   IDoc Message Mappings

This section will introduce examples of how to handle the XML-IDoc message mappings inside SAP NetWeaver PI, including different types of mappings and optimizing their structures for testing.

5.14.1   Optimizing the IDoc's Structure

When you test very large IDocs in the message mapping, you may notice that sometimes it takes a very long time to load large IDocs and debug them via mapping queues. This happens because the metadata description of large IDocs can become very large.

The XSD description of an IDoc has many fields such as the ones shown in Listing 5.4.

```
<?xml version="1.0" encoding="ISO-8859-1"?>
<xsd:schema xmlns:xsd="http://www.w3.org/2001/XMLSchema">
<xsd:element name="MATMAS05">
<xsd:complexType>
<xsd:sequence>
<xsd:element name="IDOC" type="MATMAS.MATMAS05" />
</xsd:sequence>
</xsd:complexType>
</xsd:element>
<xsd:complexType name="MATMAS05.E1MPOPM">
<xsd:annotation>
<xsd:documentation>
  Master material forecast parameter
</xsd:documentation>
</xsd:annotation>
<xsd:sequence>
<xsd:element name="MSGFN" minOccurs="0">
<xsd:annotation>
<xsd:documentation> Function </xsd:documentation>
</xsd:annotation>
<xsd:simpleType>
<xsd:restriction base="xsd:string">
<xsd:maxLength value="3" />
</xsd:restriction>
</xsd:simpleType>
</xsd:element>
<xsd:element name="VERSP" minOccurs="0">
<xsd:annotation>
<xsd:documentation>
  Version number of forecast parameters
</xsd:documentation>
</xsd:annotation>
<xsd:simpleType>
<xsd:restriction base="xsd:string">
<xsd:maxLength value="2" />
```

```
</xsd:restriction>
</xsd:simpleType>
```

Listing 5.4 An IDoc's Full MATMAS05 XSD Description

When working with testing of large IDocs, on the message mapping's TEST tab, you can reduce this structure to improve testing performance. After you import the IDoc into the Integration Repository, you can export its reduced structure. To accomplish this, follow these steps:

1. Open the standard IDoc, select EXPORT REDUCED XSD from the TOOLS menu (see Figure 5.72), and save the file in your file system with an XSD extension.

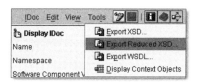

Figure 5.72 Exporting a Reduced IDoc

2. Next, you need to import the file (see Figure 5.73) as a new external definition in the INTERFACE OBJECTS tree by changing the CATEGORY to XSD and selecting the previously generated FILE.

Figure 5.73 Importing a Reduced IDoc's Definition

3. If you open your new structure, you will see that its description is greatly reduced, as shown in Listing 5.5.

```
<?xml version="1.0" encoding="ISO-8859-1"?>
<xsd:schema xmlns:xsd="http://www.w3.org/2001/XMLSchema">
<xsd:element name="MATMAS05">
<xsd:complexType>
<xsd:sequence>
<xsd:element name="IDOC" type="MATMAS.MATMAS05" />
</xsd:sequence>
</xsd:complexType>
</xsd:element>
```

```
<xsd:complexType name="MATMAS05.E1MPOPM">
<xsd:sequence>
<xsd:element name="MSGFN" minOccurs="0" />
<xsd:element name="VERSP" minOccurs="0" />
<xsd:element name="PROPR" minOccurs="0" />
<xsd:element name="MODAW" minOccurs="0" />
<xsd:element name="MODAV" minOccurs="0" />
<xsd:element name="KZPAR" minOccurs="0" />
<xsd:element name="OPGRA" minOccurs="0" />
<xsd:element name="KZINI" minOccurs="0" />
```

Listing 5.5 A Reduced IDoc's MATMAS05 XSD Description

You can use the reduced IDoc to test the message mappings for all of your large testing cases but be careful: The new message does not contain full information. This is why it should only be used in mapping tests.

5.14.2 Message Mapping Examples

Mapping IDocs to other data formats is not always an easy task. SAP NetWeaver PI offers four different ways of creating the mapping programs, as follows:

▶ Graphical message mapping

▶ XSLT mappings (on both Java and ABAP stacks)

▶ Java mappings

▶ ABAP mappings

The first two options are very easy to use. Some XSLT mappings can even be taken directly from other mapping tools. Java or ABAP mappings should be used only when there is no other way to do the mapping.

IDoc structures usually contain many identifiers, describing qualities such as type of material, type of date, type of organizational structure, and so on. You can find sample segments with their identifiers in the appendix of this book. Many other data formats do not contain this many identifiers. This is why two of the most prevalent mapping issues are how to extract necessary data from an IDoc using the identifier and how to create an IDoc segment with the identifier from a message that does not contain any identifiers. The following examples show you how to handle segments that have identifiers, using graphical message mappings and XSLT mappings.

5.14.3   Graphical Message Mapping

First, you will try to extract data from an IDoc segment using graphical message mapping and placing it into a flatter XML structure. Follow these steps:

1. You will use data from segment E1EDKA1, which contains partner data (see the appendix for details on this segment). Listing 5.6 shows a portion of a sample IDoc with data in segment E1EDKA1.

```
[...]
 <E1EDKA1 SEGMENT="">
   <PARVW>AG</PARVW>
   <PARTN>4000</PARTN>
   <LIFNR/>
   <NAME1/>
   <NAME2/>
   <NAME3/>
   <NAME4/>
[...]
 </E1EDKA1>
 <E1EDKA1 SEGMENT="">
   <PARVW>WE</PARVW>
   <PARTN>3000</PARTN>
   <LIFNR/>
   <NAME1/>
   <NAME2/>
   <NAME3/>
   <NAME4/>
 </E1EDKA1>
[...]
```

Listing 5.6 Portion of a Sample IDoc with Partner Data

2. The AG identifier specifies the SOLD-TO PARTY partner and the WE identifier the SHIP-TO PARTY values. The target message from Listing 5.7 does not have any identifiers, just two tags: one for the customer and one for the ship-to party.

```
<TargetMessage>
<Header>
  <Customer>4000</Customer>
  <ShipToParty>3000</ShipToParty>
</Header>
</TargetMessage>
```

Listing 5.7 XML Message Used for Mapping Exercises

3. To start the mapping, you need to create a message type of type `TargetMessage` and import the IDoc `ORDERS05`. You can import IDocs as shown in Section 5.4.

4. To create a message type of type `TargetMessage`, you first need to create a data type with the same structure as the sample target XML message. You then use this data type during the creation of the message type. Then you need to create a new message mapping and insert a source message (IDoc `ORDERS05`) and a target message (our new `TargetMessage` structure). Figure 5.74 shows a sample message mapping with both input and output structures filled in.

The message mapping allows you to use many standard functions that will help you create this mapping without a single line of code.

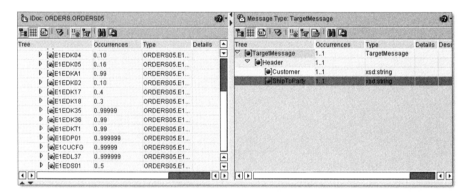

Figure 5.74 Message Mapping

5. To map the IDoc to a flatter XML structure, you need to create a mapping algorithm. You need to map a value from the PARTN tag (see Listing 5.6) from segment E1EDKA1 to the target value `Customer` (see Listing 5.7) only when the value of PARVW is equal to AG. The target SHIPTOPARTY field needs to be filled when PARVW is equal to WE. Several predefined functions will allow you to do this very easily.

- **"equals" from the Text function group**
  This function checks whether the two compared strings are equal.

- **"ifWithoutElse" from the Boolean function group**
  This function returns the value of the second argument when the first argument will return `true`.

- **"Constant" from the Constants function group**
  You can use this function to return any constant value.

▷ **"removeContext" from the Node function group**

This will delete all hierarchy levels (context changes) that the preceding function returned.

Using these functions, you can create the target mapping as shown in Figure 5.75 for the SHIPToPARTY element. This element will only enter the value of the partner number (PARTN) when the identifier (PARVW) is equal to WE.

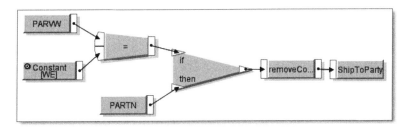

Figure 5.75 Ship-to Party Mapping

6. By changing the target value to CUSTOMER and changing the Constant value to AG, you can use the same mapping for the customer target element.

7. You can test the mapping on the TEST tab of the message mapping by filling the IDoc structure with some values for the E1EDKA1 segment and starting the test with the TEST button. Your result should be similar to the one shown in Figure 5.76.

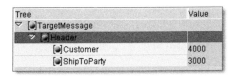

Figure 5.76 Message Mapping Test

5.14.4 User-Defined Functions in Graphical Message Mapping

Graphical message mapping is very easy, but if the logic becomes more complex, it becomes difficult to process all of these blocks. Graphical message mapping, on the other hand, provides you with special user-defined functions (created from the message mapping menu) that can help reduce the number of blocks in the mapping. In this section, you will use an advanced function to achieve the same target message mapping.

There are two types of user-defined functions: simple and advanced. The main difference is that the advanced functions can import not only individual field values but also the entire structure — all PARTN values and not just one — and they can also return many values, rather than just a single one.

1. You can create an advanced user-defined function in the message mapping and then select its properties, as shown in Figure 5.77. Use the following values:

    ▷ **Label**
    Lets you enter a name for the new function.

    ▷ **Description**
    Lets you enter a description of how the function will be used.

    ▷ **Cache**
    Lets you distinguish between simple functions (VALUE) and advanced functions (CONTEXT and QUEUE). The difference between CONTEXT and QUEUE is that CONTEXT returns only the values from the XML tree that is being processed, and QUEUE returns values from the entire XML document. The QUEUE option is much more memory-intensive and should not be used unless necessary.

    ▷ **Arguments**
    Lets you enter the names of the arguments that will be accessed in the function's code.

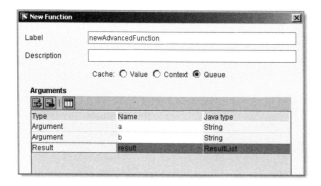

Figure 5.77 Creating an Advanced User-Defined Function

2. In our example, you only need two arguments: one for the PARTN element and one for the PARVW element. After the function has been created, a simple Java editor opens (see Figure 5.78) where you can write the code for the function.

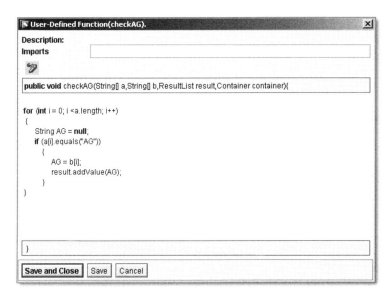

Figure 5.78 Java Editor in the Message Mapping

3. The code in our scenario will be a very simple `for`-loop on an array that holds all PARVW values. If the value is equal to AG, you will take it from the array of PARTN elements and return it from the function via the RESULTLIST object. RE-SULTLIST is used in advanced functions to return the results of the function.

4. You can create the same function for partner type WE, or you can create a more dynamic function that will take one more parameter (constant WE or AG). Therefore, you will be able to reuse the function just by changing the constant value.

Testing the new function can be done the same way as in the previous case: from the TEST tab of the message mapping.

5.14.5 XSLT Message Mapping

There are cases, however, when graphical message mapping is not suitable or when creating the mapping with this technique would produce a result that would be unreadable for developers. SAP NetWeaver PI enables you to use many other mapping techniques and one of the most widely known is *XSLT mappings*. *Extensible Stylesheet Language Transformations (XSLT)* is a globally known standard mapping language that can easily be incorporated to work with SAP NetWeaver PI.

There is no XSLT editor in the Integration Repository, but you can create XSLT mappings using other free or commercial XSLT mapping tools and import the mapping into the Integration Repository.

1. This section will provide you with the information on how to achieve exactly the same result obtained with the message mapping in the previous section by using the XSLT mappings shown in Listing 5.8.

```
<?xml version='1.0' ?>
<xsl:stylesheet version="1.0" xmlns:xsl="http://www.w3.org/1999/XSL/
Transform">
<xsl:template match="/">
<TargetMessage>
<Header>
<xsl:for-each select="ORDERS05/IDOC/E1EDKA1">
<xsl:if test="PARVW = 'AG'">
<Customer>
<xsl:value-of select="PARTN"/>
</Customer>
</xsl:if>
</xsl:for-each>
<xsl:for-each select="ORDERS05/IDOC/E1EDKA1">
<xsl:if test="PARVW = 'WE'">
<ShipToParty>
<xsl:value-of select="PARTN"/>
</ShipToParty>
</xsl:if>
</xsl:for-each>
</Header>
</TargetMessage>
</xsl:template>
</xsl:stylesheet>
```

Listing 5.8 XSLT Mapping

2. The XSLT mapping in Listing 5.8 uses several standard XSLT functions, as follows:

 ▶ **<xsl:for-each>**
   This element allows you to do looping in XSLT, and you can use it to check all E1EDKA1 segments for specific identifiers.

 ▶ **<xsl:if>**
   This is a standard conditional expression which specifies what to do when the condition is reached.

▷ **<xsl:value-of>**
This function can be used to extract the value of a specified element.

3. XSLT mappings need to be archived into ZIP or JAR format before they can be uploaded into the Integration Repository. After the archive has been created, it can be uploaded as an imported archive in the MAPPING OBJECTS section.

4. You need to create an interface mapping object as shown in Figure 5.79 to use and test the XSLT mappings. Interface mapping objects allow you to select the type of mapping you need to use. If you want to use XSLT mappings, you need to select mapping TYPE XSL and then select the name of the mapping by using search help on the mapping's NAME field.

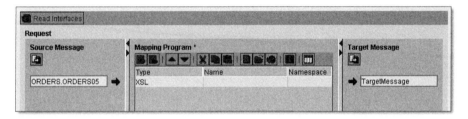

Figure 5.79 Interface Mapping

5. XSLT mappings can be tested only on the interface mapping's TEST tab, and the result should be exactly the same as using graphical message mapping.

The next section will walk you through a similar example but in the opposite direction; this time, the IDOC will be the target structure.

5.14.6 Graphical Message Mapping

The second scenario involves the same messages but the mapping will be done in the other direction. You will create an IDoc message segment with identifiers from a flat XML structure.

1. To achieve this using a graphical message mapping, you will use a few user functions. The first one will return two values—AG and WE—and it will be used twice. The code for this function can be found in Listing 5.9.

```
result.addValue("AG");
result.addValue("WE");
```

Listing 5.9 Advanced User-Defined Function addAGandWE

2. The function will be used twice because you first need to create two segments E1EDKA1 (one for the CUSTOMER and one for the SHIPTOPARTY) during the mapping execution. Figure 5.80 shows how to connect a user-defined function with the target element.

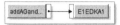

Figure 5.80 Creating Two Segments

3. Next, you can use the same function addAGandWE to create two elements PARVW with values AG and WE. Because they will be in different segments, you need to use standard function SplitByValue from the NODE functions group to create a context change after each new element (see Figure 5.81).

Figure 5.81 Creating Two PARVW Elements

4. Then, you need to create a new function sortAGandWE (see Listing 5.10), which will have two input values—CUSTOMER and SHIPTOPARTY—and will return them one by one.

```
result.addValue(a[0]);
result.addValue(b[0]);
```

Listing 5.10 Advanced User-Defined Function sortAGandWE

5. Because the values are also in different segments, you need to use the Split-ByValue function again, as shown in Figure 5.82.

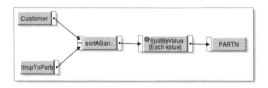

Figure 5.82 Graphical Message Mapping

6. This is enough to create two E1EDKA1 segments for the IDoc with different identifiers.

The same example can also be performed using XSLT mappings. We will describe this in the next section.

5.14.7 XSLT Mapping

The XSLT code for the same scenario looks much simpler because you only have to use one `<xsl:value-of>` function to create all of the necessary segments of the IDoc (see Listing 5.11).

```
<?xml version='1.0' ?>
<xsl:stylesheet version="1.0" xmlns:xsl="http://www.w3.org/1999/XSL/
Transform">
<xsl:template match="/">
<ORDERS05>
<IDOC>
<E1EDKA1>
<PARVW>AG</PARVW>
<PARTN>
<xsl:value-of select="TargetMessage/Header/Customer"/>
</PARTN>
</E1EDKA1>
<E1EDKA1>
<PARVW>WE</PARVW>
<PARTN>
<xsl:value-of select="TargetMessage/Header/ShipToParty"/>
</PARTN>
</E1EDKA1>
</IDOC>
</ORDERS05>
</xsl:template>
</xsl:stylesheet>
```

Listing 5.11 XSLT Mapping

The amount of time needed to prepare your mappings with different mapping programs will depend heavily on your experience and the tools you can use. One thing you should remember is that XSLT mappings are transportable programs that can be used with different tools, including those provided by different vendors. Furthermore, you should use Java and ABAP mappings only when necessary because developers find these types of mappings less readable than graphical message mappings or XSLT mappings.

5.15   Enabling ABAP Proxies From Every Outbound IDoc

One of the latest communication methods supported by SAP application systems is sending and receiving XML data using the HTTP protocol. SAP application systems support this if they are based on the SAP Web Application Server 6.20 or higher. To send or receive a message via HTTP, application systems use what are called ABAP proxy messages—that is, messages sent/received using ABAP proxies. In simple terms, ABAP proxies are a set of classes (and methods) generated automatically from an SAP NetWeaver PI's message interface that you develop inside the NetWeaver PI's Integration Repository. Methods of these classes allow either sending a message to SAP NetWeaver PI or receiving a message from the middleware. When compared to IDoc messages, ABAP proxies offer a set of advantages:

▶ ABAP proxy messages do not use the RFC protocol that is known only to SAP applications. Instead, they use the HTTP protocol known to many more applications.

▶ ABAP proxy messages are not designed in SAP application systems but in the middleware (inside SAP NetWeaver PI as a message interface). All structures, tables, and fields inside SAP application systems are automatically generated and ready to be used—thus, you have one place where you store all of your message structures instead of having them in each SAP application system (such as ERP, SCM, or CRM).

▶ ABAP proxy messages exchange XML messages so they do not have to be converted inside SAP NetWeaver PI from IDoc format to XML and vice versa before SAP NetWeaver PI can process them (as SAP NetWeaver PI can only process XML messages internally).

It is also true that SAP has prepared many ABAP proxy messages especially for a set of new applications (e.g., SAP Auto-ID Infrastructure) where IDoc interfaces are no longer in use.

Is there a way then to send information from all IDocs as ABAP proxy messages? The simplest answer is that there is not and if you would like to use the new protocol for a message that exists only as an IDoc interface, you need to carry out the entire development on your own. That would mean not only creating the message as a container but also finding a way (user exit, BAdI, etc.) through which the ABAP proxy message can be sent and, most important, finding (selecting) the data to fill the new message. But is there really no way to use the data prepared in IDoc messages and send it using an ABAP proxy message?

It turns out that a nice workaround exists, which allows sending every outbound IDoc as an ABAP proxy message. For this you will use a special port, as shown in Figure 1.8 of Section 1.2, called ABAP Programming Interface (ABAP PI). This port allows specifying a destination that is a function module created in an SAP Application system. From this function module, you will be sending ABAP proxy messages created from IDoc data. The function module specified in this port will receive an IDoc's control record as input, which contains the IDoc number among other data. Later, you can use this IDoc number to retrieve the IDoc data and populate ABAP proxy messages from this data. This approach can be very useful for many reasons. The most important are:

▶ You do not need to select the data from the database because you have all of the information inside the IDoc.

▶ IDocs have a predefined structure and you can easily find out what kind of data they provide using Transaction WE60 (IDoc documentation).

▶ You do not have to look for any special user exits from which you could send the proxy message because you can easily do so inside the function module specified in the port. This will work for all IDocs, which is not the case with a user exit, for example (because most applications have user exists in different places).

To summarize the concept of this workaround approach: You can send any IDoc to a special port, which will point to a function module. From this function module, you can retrieve IDoc data, populate the ABAP proxy message with this data, and send the ABAP proxy message.

You need to perform three steps to prepare a sample scenario, as follows:

1. You need to create a message interface inside SAP NetWeaver PI.

2. You need to generate ABAP proxy classes and methods from this message interface inside the SAP application system.

3. You need to create a new function module that will retrieve IDoc data, populate an ABAP proxy message using this data, and send the message.

Before you can start with the development, you need to make sure that your SAP application is ABAP proxy-enabled. To do so, you need to check whether the SAP application system is based on at least on SAP Web AS 6.20 (kernel patch level 1253, check SAP Note 675441 and 721160 for more information) and whether the SAP application system is connected with SAP NetWeaver PI. Connecting the SAP application system with SAP NetWeaver PI is beyond the scope of this book; therefore, we will only mention the necessary configuration steps without describing them further:

▸ Registering the SAP application system's technical system in the SLD using Transaction RZ70, described in Section 5.3.1.

▸ Creating a business system for the SAP application system's client, which is also described in Section 5.3.2.

▸ Creating an RFC destination of type HTTP, pointing to the SAP NetWeaver PI system that will be used in Transaction SXMB_ADM (Integration Engine Configuration).

▸ Defining an SAP application system as the APPLICATION SYSTEM in Transaction SXMB_ADM.

▸ Registering the queues in Transaction SXMB_ADM (Queue Registration).

▸ Defining the connection between the SAP application system and the SLD. This consists of creating two RFC destinations (LCRSAPRFC and SAPSLDAPI) and maintenance of Transaction SLDAPICUST.

This configuration needs to be done on SAP application systems only. It can be checked using Transaction SLDCHECK. If executing this transaction results in only green messages, then ABAP proxy communication should be enabled and you can proceed to the actual development of the solution.

SAP NetWeaver PI Development

As mentioned in the overview of the solution, to generate an ABAP proxy message, you need to create a message interface. Before you can do so, you need to create two lower level objects—a message type (on which the message interface is based) and a data type (on which the message type is based). You can create these objects in any of your customer software component versions and here, we assume that you have already created one in the SLD and imported it into the Integration Repository. Our proxy does not need to have all IDocs fields because it is just an example. Therefore, you start with creating a new data type with three fields. You will then send a delivery IDoc as an ABAP proxy. This IDoc's configuration was explained in Section 2.6. For this exercise you will use only the following three fields:

▶ DELIVERY—number of the outbound delivery

▶ SOLDTO—buyer's partner number

▶ SHIPTO—number of the buyer's location to which the goods will be delivered

After you right-click the DATA TYPE node in the software component version, you can create a new data type named DT_IDOC_PROXY, as shown in Figure 5.83. Because you will be using a custom-developed program, make sure you use the same names or remember to change them appropriately later on in the code sample.

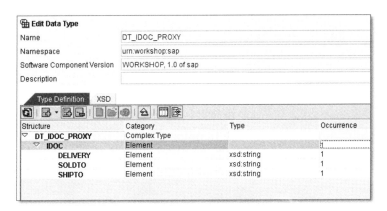

Figure 5.83 Data Type for an IDoc ABAP Proxy Message

After you save the data type, you need to create the message type MT_IDOC_PROXY. You do this the same way (right-click the MESSAGE TYPE node). Message types are based on data types; therefore, you just need to select the data type DT_IDOC_ PROXY in the DATA TYPE USED field, as shown in Figure 5.84.

The last and most important thing you need to create inside the SAP NetWeaver PI Integration Repository is the message interface. The message interface is the object in which you not only specify the message type used but also the mode (synchronous for messages in which you expect a response message or asynchronous for message without any response—e.g., IDocs) and the category:

▶ **Inbound**

Used for messages sent by SAP NetWeaver PI (thus, they are inbound in terms of the application system).

▶ **Outbound**

Used for messages received by SAP NetWeaver PI (these are outbound in terms of the application system).

▶ **Abstract**

These are message interfaces used only in integration processes or SAP NetWeaver PI.

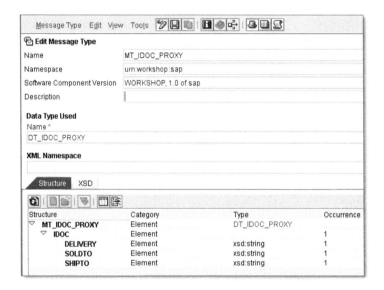

Figure 5.84 Message Type Used for an IDoc ABAP Proxy Message

This is why in our case, the message interface MI_IDOC_PROXY_AO will be an outbound message and asynchronous, as shown in Figure 5.85 (AO at the end of the message interface describes the category and mode).

After you activate all saved objects on the CHANGE tab of the Integration Repository, you are finished with the development of SAP NetWeaver PI objects. We will not describe how you can specify the receiver of the message in the Integration Directory because we only want to show how you can send an ABAP proxy message to an SAP NetWeaver PI system. The Integration Directory configuration here is exactly the same as for any other flow.

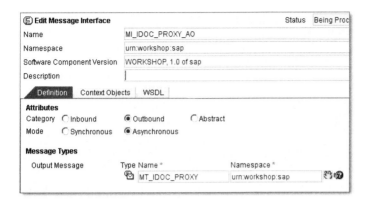

Figure 5.85 Asynchronous and Outbound Message Interface

SAP Application System Development

If the message interface is prepared in SAP NetWeaver PI and an SAP application system is connected with SAP NetWeaver PI, opening Transaction SPROXY on the SAP application system will show all message interfaces from SAP NetWeaver PI. If you are using SAP ERP 2006 or higher, you need to know that the names of SAP NetWeaver PI objects inside the SAP application system have the names from SAP NetWeaver PI 7.1; this is why SAP NetWeaver PI message interfaces can be found under the node SERVICE INTERFACES (this is the new term for message interfaces). Before you can generate an ABAP proxy, you need to create a package inside Transaction SE80 using the CREATE NEW PACKAGE option. Call the package ZBOOK. When you right-click MI_IDOC_PROXY_AO, you will see an option to create the proxy object, as shown in Figure 5.86.

Figure 5.86 Creating a Proxy

When you select this option, you will be asked for a package (ZBOOK) and a prefix (ZIDOC)—this can be anything starting with Z or Y, as do all SAP customer objects. You can also assign the proxy to a transport request. A completed screen is shown in Figure 5.87.

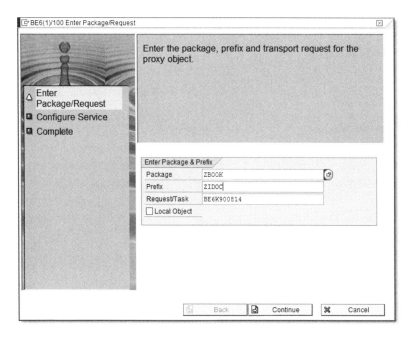

Figure 5.87 Proxy Generation—Package and Prefix assignment

Clicking the CONTINUE button starts the generation of the proxy message. If everything is generated correctly, you can activate all generated objects afterwards. If this is not the case (there are error messages), go back to creating a data type and carefully repeat the procedure.

The next thing you need to do is create the new function module that will be sending the ABAP proxy messages. There is a predefined function called OWN_FUNCTION that you can copy in Transaction SE37 to a customer function (with a Z or Y prefix). Next, you can modify the function's code so that it will retrieve IDoc data (the three fields discussed earlier) and send the ABAP proxy message. You can find the entire function module's code in Listing 5.12. It contains some parts of the original code of function OWN_FUCNTION, together with the necessary coding for sending the ABAP proxy message. For details on how the function works, take a look at the comments in the listing.

```
FUNCTION Z_OWN_FUNCTION.
*"----------------------------------------------------------------
-
*"*"Lokalny interfejs:
```

```
*"  TABLES
*"      I_EDIDC STRUCTURE  EDIDC
*"------------------------------------------------------------------
-
TABLES: EDIDC, EDI_DS.
DATA: BEGIN OF I_EDIDD OCCURS 0.
        INCLUDE STRUCTURE EDIDD.
DATA: END OF I_EDIDD.
DATA: ERROR(1).
LOOP AT I_EDIDC.
*first, you need to open the IDOC and read it
  CALL FUNCTION 'EDI_DOCUMENT_OPEN_FOR_PROCESS'
       EXPORTING
*          DB_READ_OPTION          = DB_READ
           DOCUMENT_NUMBER         = I_EDIDC-DOCNUM
*          ENQUEUE_OPTION          = SYNCHRONOUS
       IMPORTING
           IDOC_CONTROL            = EDIDC
       EXCEPTIONS
           DOCUMENT_FOREIGN_LOCK   = 1
           DOCUMENT_NOT_EXIST      = 2
           DOCUMENT_NUMBER_INVALID = 3
           DOCUMENT_IS_ALREADY_OPEN = 4
           OTHERS                  = 5.
  IF SY-SUBRC <> 0.
    MESSAGE ID SY-MSGID TYPE SY-MSGTY NUMBER SY-MSGNO
            WITH SY-MSGV1 SY-MSGV2 SY-MSGV3 SY-MSGV4.
  ENDIF.
  CLEAR I_EDIDD.
  REFRESH I_EDIDD.
  CALL FUNCTION 'EDI_SEGMENTS_GET_ALL'
       EXPORTING
           DOCUMENT_NUMBER         = I_EDIDC-DOCNUM
       TABLES
           IDOC_CONTAINERS         = I_EDIDD
       EXCEPTIONS
           DOCUMENT_NUMBER_INVALID = 1
           END_OF_DOCUMENT         = 2
           OTHERS                  = 3.
  IF SY-SUBRC <> 0.
    MESSAGE ID SY-MSGID TYPE SY-MSGTY NUMBER SY-MSGNO
            WITH SY-MSGV1 SY-MSGV2 SY-MSGV3 SY-MSGV4.
```

```
  ENDIF.
  ERROR = 'N'.
DATA: C_E1EDL20(10) TYPE C VALUE 'E1EDL20'.
DATA: C_E1ADRM1(10) TYPE C VALUE 'E1ADRM1'.
DATA: LS_E1EDL20 type E1EDL20.
DATA: LS_E1ADRM1 type E1ADRM1.
DATA: LV_DELIVERY type vbeln.
DATA: LV_SOLDTO type KUNAG.
DATA: LV_SHIPTO type KUNWE.
*now you can loop on the IDOC data to retrieve the data you need
loop at I_EDIDD.
CASE I_EDIDD-SEGNAM.
WHEN C_E1EDL20.
LS_E1EDL20 = I_EDIDD-SDATA.
LV_DELIVERY = LS_E1EDL20-VBELN.
WHEN C_E1ADRM1.
LS_E1ADRM1 = I_EDIDD-SDATA.
if LS_E1ADRM1-PARTNER_Q = 'AG'.
LV_SOLDTO = LS_E1ADRM1-PARTNER_ID.
elseif LS_E1ADRM1-PARTNER_Q = 'WE'.
LV_SHIPTO = LS_E1ADRM1-PARTNER_ID.
else.
endif.
endcase.
endloop.
*after you have the data you need, you can call the proxy
DATA prxy1 TYPE REF TO ZIDOCCO_MI_IDOC_PROXY_AO.
CREATE OBJECT prxy1.
DATA: it_IDOC type ZIDOCMT_IDOC_PROXY.
try.
it_IDOC-MT_IDOC_PROXY-IDOC-DELIVERY = LV_DELIVERY.
it_IDOC-MT_IDOC_PROXY-IDOC-SOLDTO = LV_SOLDTO .
it_IDOC-MT_IDOC_PROXY-IDOC-SHIPTO = LV_SHIPTO .
*you call the proxy using a method which has the same
*name as the message interface—in some older releases (< ECC 6.0)
*you used another method: call_asynchronous
    CALL METHOD prxy1->MI_IDOC_PROXY_AO
      EXPORTING
        output = it_IDOC.
    commit work

    .
  CATCH cx_ai_system_fault .
```

```
    DATA fault1 TYPE REF TO cx_ai_system_fault .
    CREATE OBJECT fault1.
    WRITE :/ fault1->errortext.
endtry.
*depending on the call result, you can set the status
*of the original IDoc so that any errors will be visible in
*Transaction WE02
  CLEAR EDI_DS.
  EDI_DS-DOCNUM = I_EDIDC-DOCNUM.
  EDI_DS-TABNAM = 'EDI_DS'.
  EDI_DS-LOGDAT = SY-DATUM.
  EDI_DS-LOGTIM = SY-UZEIT.
  EDI_DS-REPID = 'OWN_FUNCTION'.
  IF ERROR = 'Y'.
    EDI_DS-STATUS = '20'.
    EDI_DS-STAMQU = 'SAP'.
*   edi_ds-stamid = Fehlernummern-ID
*   edi_ds-stamno = Fehlernummer
*   edi_ds-stapa1 = 1. Parameter
*   edi_ds-stapa2 = 2. Parameter
*   edi_ds-stapa3 = 3. Parameter
*   edi_ds-stapa4 = 4. Parameter
    CALL FUNCTION 'EDI_DOCUMENT_STATUS_SET'
        EXPORTING
             DOCUMENT_NUMBER          = I_EDIDC-DOCNUM
             IDOC_STATUS              = EDI_DS
*       IMPORTING
*            IDOC_CONTROL             =
        EXCEPTIONS
             DOCUMENT_NUMBER_INVALID = 1
             OTHER_FIELDS_INVALID    = 2
             STATUS_INVALID          = 3
             OTHERS                  = 4.
    IF SY-SUBRC <> 0.
      MESSAGE ID SY-MSGID TYPE SY-MSGTY NUMBER SY-MSGNO
             WITH SY-MSGV1 SY-MSGV2 SY-MSGV3 SY-MSGV4.
    ENDIF.
    CALL FUNCTION 'IDOC_ERROR_WORKFLOW_START'
        EXPORTING
             DOCNUM                   = I_EDIDC-DOCNUM
             EVENTCODE                = 'EDIO'
*            MESS                     = ' '
```

```
      EXCEPTIONS
            NO_ENTRY_IN_TEDE5       = 1
            ERROR_IN_START_WORKFLOW = 2
            OTHERS                  = 3.
   IF SY-SUBRC <> 0.
     MESSAGE ID SY-MSGID TYPE SY-MSGTY NUMBER SY-MSGNO
            WITH SY-MSGV1 SY-MSGV2 SY-MSGV3 SY-MSGV4.
   ENDIF.
 ELSE.
   EDI_DS-STATUS = '18'.
   EDI_DS-STAMQU = 'SAP'.
*  edi_ds-stamid = Fehlernummern-ID
*  edi_ds-stamno = Fehlernummer
*  edi_ds-stapa1 = 1. Parameter
*  edi_ds-stapa2 = 2. Parameter
*  edi_ds-stapa3 = 3. Parameter
*  edi_ds-stapa4 = 4. Parameter
   CALL FUNCTION 'EDI_DOCUMENT_STATUS_SET'
        EXPORTING
            DOCUMENT_NUMBER         = I_EDIDC-DOCNUM
            IDOC_STATUS             = EDI_DS
*       IMPORTING
*            IDOC_CONTROL            =
        EXCEPTIONS
            DOCUMENT_NUMBER_INVALID = 1
            OTHER_FIELDS_INVALID    = 2
            STATUS_INVALID          = 3
            OTHERS                  = 4.
   IF SY-SUBRC <> 0.
     MESSAGE ID SY-MSGID TYPE SY-MSGTY NUMBER SY-MSGNO
            WITH SY-MSGV1 SY-MSGV2 SY-MSGV3 SY-MSGV4.
   ENDIF.
 ENDIF.
 CALL FUNCTION 'EDI_DOCUMENT_CLOSE_PROCESS'
      EXPORTING
            DOCUMENT_NUMBER    = I_EDIDC-DOCNUM
*           BACKGROUND         = NO_BACKGROUND
*           NO_DEQUEUE         = ' '
*      IMPORTING
*            IDOC_CONTROL       =
      EXCEPTIONS
            DOCUMENT_NOT_OPEN  = 1
```

```
              FAILURE_IN_DB_WRITE = 2
              PARAMETER_ERROR     = 3
              STATUS_SET_MISSING  = 4
              OTHERS              = 5.
   IF SY-SUBRC <> 0.
     MESSAGE ID SY-MSGID TYPE SY-MSGTY NUMBER SY-MSGNO
              WITH SY-MSGV1 SY-MSGV2 SY-MSGV3 SY-MSGV4.
   ENDIF.
 ENDLOOP.
 ENDFUNCTION.
```

Listing 5.12 Function for Sending ABAP Proxy Messages from IDoc

Next, you need to create the new port in Transaction WE21, where you specify the function module. Select the ABAP-PI node and click the CREATE button (F7) inside Transaction WE21. Then, enter a description and the new function module for sending ABAP proxy messages into the respective fields and save (see Figure 5.88).

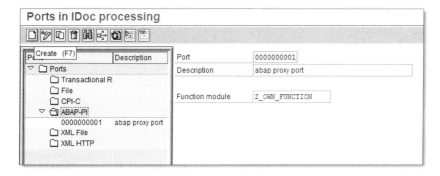

Figure 5.88 Port with a Function Module for Sending ABAP Proxy Messages

Because the IDoc configuration for sending a delivery IDoc was already explained in Chapter 2, Section 2.6, and the only change you need to make is selecting the new port as described in Section 2.6.4, "Defining the Partner Profile," you are ready to test the scenario.

Testing Sending an ABAP Proxy Message from an IDoc Message

Testing the message involves creating a delivery. This is not shown here but if the delivery IDoc was created, the ABAP proxy message should have been created as well. You can check this in Transaction SXI_MONITOR of the SAP application system (not yet in SAP NetWeaver PI). If you used the code provided, the message should be similar to the one shown in Figure 5.89 (the numbers of delivery and partners will be different).

```xml
<?xml version="1.0" encoding="utf-8" ?>
- <MT_IDOC_PROXY xmlns:prx="urn:sap.com:proxy:BE6:/1SAI/TASE51903B9C74BF633C891:700:2008/06/25">
  - <IDOC>
      <DELIVERY>0080000001</DELIVERY>
      <SOLDTO>000000001</SOLDTO>
      <SHIPTO>000000001</SHIPTO>
    </IDOC>
  </MT_IDOC_PROXY>
```

Figure 5.89 ABAP Proxy Message Created from an IDoc

Whether the ABAP proxy call was successful or unsuccessful, you should see an IDoc message in Transaction WE02 (for IDoc monitoring, refer to Chapter 4). If everything was correct, the IDoc should have a green status, if there was an error, the IDoc status should be red.

As you can see, this is not a standard approach to send ABAP proxy messages from IDocs. However, because this is not a very well known solution, we decided to describe it in detail, taking into consideration both the benefits of using ABAP proxy messages as well as the sometimes occurring necessity of using ABAP proxy messages in some business scenarios. The scenario described also provides a good example of using the ABAP-PI port. This does not have to be used only for sending ABAP proxy messages; we're sure you will find other solutions in which knowledge of this type of port will come in handy.

5.16   Summary

After reading this chapter, you should be able to configure SAP NetWeaver PI to send and receive IDoc messages properly, and to create more advanced IDoc flows involving scheduling, IDoc acknowledgments, and IDoc serialization.

The mapping examples provided in this chapter should make you familiar with using different mapping types and help you leverage standard and user-defined functions with the most popular type of mapping, graphical message mapping.

6   Summary

SAP application integration can be implemented very smoothly once you thoroughly understand the tools that support integration projects. IDocs—one of the most popular SAP interfaces—run in almost all large SAP system environments. With the information in this book, you should now be able to configure many IDoc scenarios, enhance them with advanced Message Control, and administer them. This second edition of the book provides you with information on not only several new functionalities developed within the latest enhancement packages (such as the new IDoc packaging) but also on new ideas for using IDoc interfaces with ABAP proxies, for example.

SAP NetWeaver PI is the standard middleware tool used to connect SAP applications with the outside world. It supports the use of new protocols, such as SOAP and XML, and standards, such as RosettaNet. This book showed you not only how to connect SAP NetWeaver PI with SAP application systems via IDoc interfaces but also how to optimize flows using message bundling and IDoc reduction. You learned how to monitor IDoc flows within SAP NetWeaver PI and by using SAP Solution Manager. In addition, you learned how to create simple mappings: message mappings and XSLT mappings.

Because most examples were shown as step-by-step procedures, any reader who has access to the tools mentioned in the book should have been able to perform all of the exercises easily. By building a flow from the SAP application system to SAP NetWeaver PI, you are now prepared for a successful, real-life integration project. If this is the case, then we have done our job.

A   Tables

The following tables show the most popular segments of IDoc `ORDERS05`, with all of the identifiers and descriptions that are commonly used in all types of mappings.

Identifier	Description
001	Business area
002	Sales area
003	Delivering company code
004	Plant in charge
005	Delivering plant
006	Division
007	Distribution channel
008	Sales organization
009	Purchasing group
010	Sales group
011	Company code
012	Order type
013	Purchase order type
014	Purchasing organization
015	Billing type
016	Sales office
017	Unloading point
018	Quotation type
019	Purchase order type (SD)

Table A.1 IDoc ORDERS05: Segment E1EDK14

Identifier	Description
001	Delivery date (supplier)
002	Requested delivery date (customer)
003	Closing date for applications
004	Deadline for submission of quotations
005	Quotation/inquiry valid from
006	Binding period for a quotation (valid to)
007	Reconciliation date for agreed cumulative quantity
008	First firm zone
009	Second firm zone
010	Shipping date
011	Date IDoc created
012	Document date
013	Quotation date (supplier)
014	Inquiry date (customer)
015	Invoice posting date (Invoice tax point date)
016	Invoice date
017	Payment date
018	Bill of exchange date
019	Start of validity for outline agreement or inquiry
020	End of validity for outline agreement or inquiry
021	Billing date for invoice list
022	Purchase order date
023	Pricing date
024	Fixed value date
025	Created on

Table A.2 IDoc ORDERS05: Segment E1EDK03

Identifier	Description
026	Billing date for billing index and printout
027	Date on which services were rendered
028	Due date
029	Sales order date
030	Goods receipt date
031	Planned date
032	Date of reference number
033	Shipment start date
034	Planned shipment end date
035	Goods issue date
036	Bank value date
037	Bank offsetting date
038	Posting to bank
039	Ship-to party's purchase order date
040	Pickup date from (delivery order)
041	Pickup date to (delivery order)
042	Date of old balance
043	Date of new balance
044	Payment baseline date
045	Shelf-life expiration date for batch
046	Date for delivery relevance
101	Resale invoice date
102	Resale ship date
103	Booking from date
104	Booking to date

Table A.2 IDoc ORDERS05: Segment E1EDK03 (cont.)

Identifier	Description
105	Shipping from date
106	Shipping to date
107	Billing from date
108	Billing to date
109	Exercise from date
110	Exercise to date

Table A.2 IDoc ORDERS05: Segment E1EDK03 (cont.)

Identifier	Description
AA	Customer—financial document
AG	Sold-to party
AP	Contact person
AW	Shipped-to party financial document
BA	Bank sold-to party
BB	Bank beneficiary/partner for debit memo
BE	Beneficiary
BK	Company code address
CC	SPEC2000 customer code
CO	Competitors
DE	Bank holding account
EK	Buyer
I1	Sender's correspondent bank
I2	Intermediary bank
I3	Recipient's correspondent bank
I4	External house bank

Table A.3 IDoc ORDERS05: Segment E1EDKA1

Identifier	Description
LF	Vendor
LFA	Vendor for additionals
LFL	Vendor (from vendor view)
ME	Declarant
OB	Opening bank
PA	Partner for debit memo/direct debit/bank collection
RE	Invoice recipient
RG	Payer
RS	Invoicing party
SLS	Supplementary logistics service
SP	Carrier
VR	Substitute
WE	Goods recipient

Table A.3 IDoc ORDERS05: Segment E1EDKA1 (cont.)

Identifier	Description
001	Customer purchase order
002	Vendor order
003	Customer inquiry
004	Vendor quotation
005	Customer contract number
006	Vendor contract number
007	Collective number for quotations
008	Last purchase order number (SPEC2000 acknowl.)
009	Invoice number

Table A.4 IDoc ORDERS05: Segment E1EDK02

Identifier	Description
010	Internal number (document)
011	Referenced document number
011	Delivery note number
012	Internal purchase order number
013	Accounting document
014	Billing document number of invoicing party
015	Number of preceding document
017	Assignment number
018	Customer order number
019	POR number
020	Invoice list number
021	ID for cost assignment
022	Payment document number
023	Banker's acceptance
024	Matured certificate of deposit (CD)
025	Loan
026	Check number
027	Foreign exchange contract number
028	Credit memo
029	Payment advice note number
030	Original purchase order number (ALE)
031	Return leg number
032	Reference bank
033	Third-party reference number
034	Reference number of beneficiary's bank

Table A.4 IDoc ORDERS05: Segment E1EDK02 (cont.)

Identifier	Description
035	Message reference
036	Credit card number
037	Statement number
038	Account statement no. (deposit no.)
039	Account statement no. (deposit seq. no)
040	Payee code
041	MICR line
042	Imported line
043	Vendor contract number
044	Ship-to party's purchase order
045	Cost center
046	Profitability segment no.
047	Work breakdown structure object
048	Profit center
049	Business area
050	Delivery order
051	Delivery order route number
052	Sequence number
053	Scheduling agreement number
054	External transaction
055	Promotion number
056	Customer quotation number
057	Customer buying group
058	Customer contract number
059	Check number from check register

Table A.4 IDoc ORDERS05: Segment E1EDK02 (cont.)

Identifier	Description
060	JIT call number
061	Internal delivery note number
062	Customer purchase order no. for consignment issue by ext. service agent
063	External delivery note number
064	Goods receipt/issue slip number
065	Repetitive wire number
066	External order number
067	Quality notification number
068	External inquiry number
069	Business partner reference key
070	Reference text for settled items
070	Customer ID no.
071	Agreement number
072	Credit advice number
075	Check number
076	Credit posting number
077	Transfer number (just transferred)
078	Delivering profit center
079	Batch number
080	Certificate profile
081	Collective daily delivery note
082	Summarized JIT call
083	External delivering plant
084	Tax number tax office §14
101	Resale invoice no.

Table A.4 IDoc ORDERS05: Segment E1EDK02 (cont.)

Identifier	Description
102	Resale ship and debit agreement no.
103	Customer claim reference number
104	Design registration number

Table A.4 IDoc ORDERS05: Segment E1EDK02 (cont.)

Identifier	Description
001	INCOTERMS part 1
002	INCOTERMS part 2

Table A.5 IDoc ORDERS05: Segment E1EDK17

Identifier	Description
001	Payment term 1
002	Payment term 2
003	Payment term 3
004	Payment term stock transfer

Table A.6 IDoc ORDERS05: Segment E1EDK18

Identifier	Description
001	Material number used by customer
002	Material number used by vendor
003	International Article Number (EAN)
004	Manufacturer part number
005	Interchanged manufacturer part number
006	Pricing reference material
007	Commodity code
010	Batch number

Table A.7 IDoc ORDERS05: Segment E1EDP19

Identifier	Description
011	Country of origin of material
012	Shipping unit
013	Original material number (ALE)
014	Serial number
015	Manufacturing plant
016	Revision level
017	Additionals

Table A.7 IDoc ORDERS05: Segment E1EDP19 (cont.)

Identifier	Description
001	Number of items (purchase order count)
002	Net document value (EVT)
003	Gross document value
004	Total of all quantities (total control quantity)
005	Sales tax total
006	Order values
007	Sales tax
008	Invoice values
009	Target value for outline agreement
010	Net invoice value
011	Billed value
012	Amount qualifying for cash discount
013	Cash discount amount 1
014	Cash discount amount 2
015	Net values with sales tax ID

Table A.8 IDoc ORDERS05: Segment E1EDS01

Identifier	Description
016	Billed values with sales tax ID
017	Total item net value
018	Invoice list final amount
019	Net value invoice list
020	Total discounts/surcharges
021	Net weight
022	Gross weight
023	Total weight
024	Quantity of transferred materials
025	Billed value in euros
026	End amount for invoice list in euros
027	Billed value of invoice list in euros
028	Number of IDocs

Table A.8 IDoc ORDERS05: Segment E1EDS01 (cont.)

B   The authors

Michał Kowalczewski is a project manager and e-business team leader in the Business Consulting Center (Poland). The team he leads works on SAP NetWeaver corporate integration solutions, specializing in designing and implementing processes for Sales and Distribution and Customer Relationship Management. His professional interests also include mobile systems and Enterprise SOA. He graduated from Poznan University of Economics with a degree in computer science and econometrics. His master's thesis concerns semantic Web services and SOA architecture.

Michał Krawczyk received his degree in computer science and econometrics and since then has been working as an SAP integration consultant. His work focuses mainly on message exchange between SAP systems through the use of technologies such as ALE, IDocs, and SAP NetWeaver Process Integration (formerly SAP Exchange Infrastructure). Thanks to his contributions to the SAP Developer Network, he was awarded the No. 1 Contributor Award in the PI/XI area twice in 2004/2005 and 2005/2006 and once No. 2 in 2006/2007.

He has also been acting as an SAP Mentor for SDN since 2007 and is an SDN moderator. In addition, he has written articles for industry magazines such as SAP Professional Journal, SAP CRMExpert, SAP SCMExpert, SAP HRExpert, and SAP Solution Manager Expert.

Index

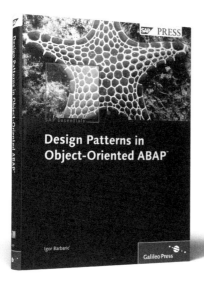

Get a detailed introduction to the concept of Design Patterns

Learn how to easily implement Singleton, Adapter, Composite, Deco-rator, Factory, Façade, and MVC

Including MVC implementation for Web Dynpro ABAP

Igor Barbaric

Design Patterns in Object-Oriented ABAP

Design patterns provide you with proven solutions for everyday coding problems. This SAP PRESS Essentials guide shows how to apply them to your favourite language: ABAP. Expanded by the implementation of the MVC pattern in Web Dynpro and a new chapter on the Factory pattern, this second edition of our programming workshop now covers all important patterns and all up-to-date ABAP techniques. Watch how the expert codes the patterns and immediately benefit from better stability and maintainability of your code!

approx. 200 pp., 2. edition, 68,– Euro / US$ 85.00
ISBN 978-1-59229-263-9, Dec 2009

>> www.sap-press.de/2018

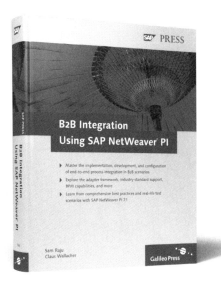

Master the implementation, development, and configuration of end-to-end process integration in B2B scenarios

Explore the adapter framework, industry-standard support, BPM capabilities, and more

Learn from comprehensive best practices and real-life test scenarios with SAP NetWeaver PI 7.1

Sam Raju, Claus Wallacher

B2B Integration Using SAP NetWeaver PI

Using SAP NetWeaver Process Integration (PI) for the implementation of B2B scenarios differs greatly from the implementation of other scenarios. This comprehensive guide for B2B process integration provides in-depth coverage: If you are an advanced to professional administrator, developer, or consultant in the PI area, you'll learn new ways to exploit SAP NetWeaver PI's integration functionality to optimize connectivity with your (global) trading partners by setting up a reliable, secure, and low-effort data exchange.

608 pp., 2008, 69,95 Euro / US$ 69.95
ISBN 978-1-59229-163-2

>> www.sap-press.de/1591

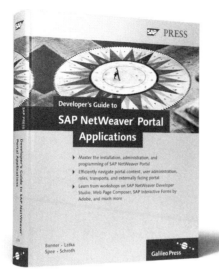

Master the installation, administration, and programming of SAP NetWeaver Portal

Efficiently navigate portal content, user administration, roles, transports, and externally facing portal

Learn from workshops on SAP NetWeaver Developer Studio, Web Page Composer, SAP Interactive Forms by Adobe, and much more

Marcus Banner, Berthold Latka, Michael Spee, Roland Schroth

Developer's Guide to SAP NetWeaver Portal Applications

From a strategic perspective, SAP NetWeaver Portal is perhaps the most important product of the SAP NetWeaver family of products. In fact, the Portal is essential to all processes within SAP NetWeaver. It serves as the fundamental platform that provides a condensed overview of all information and enables central access to all applications in the enterprise. In addition, the Portal provides the infrastructure for cooperation within and across company borders. This book provides the highly advanced functional knowledge required to correctly set up, operate, administer, and program the SAP NetWeaver Portal.

423 pp., 2008, 79,95 Euro / US$ 79.95
ISBN 978-1-59229-225-7

>> www.sap-press.de/1847

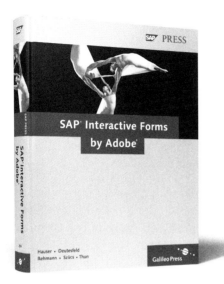

All about fundamentals, technologies, and practical solutions

Covers the usage in online and offline scenarios

With examples of Adobe Document Services, Adobe LiveCycle De-signer, ISR Framework, Web Dynpro Integration and many more

Jürgen Hauser, Andreas Deutesfeld, Stephan Rehmann, Thomas Szücs, Philipp Thun

SAP Interactive Forms by Adobe

A general introduction explains what Interactive Forms are and how they are implemented. It then illustrates the creation of print and interactive forms by the usage of technology (Adobe Document Services), via tool (Adobe LiveCycle Designer) and interface call (Web Dynpro, web service). The level of complexity of the described approaches successively increases. According to the product idea, the book covers all topics comprehensively and holistically. The knowledge transfer is supported by many screenshots and step-by-step instructions, as well as tips and tricks that will prove useful even to the advanced reader. Basic knowledge in the areas of ABAP and Web Dynpro are, however, taken for granted. There will be references to the relevant readings for acquiring the required know how at the beginning of each chapter.

approx. 624 pp., 79,95 Euro / US$ 79.95, ISBN 978-1-59229-254-7, May 2009

>> www.sap-press.de/2016

Interested in reading more?

Please visit our Web site for all
new book releases from SAP PRESS.

www.sap-press.com